The Lincoln Family Tree

William Wallace "Willie"
1850~1862

Thomas "Tad"
1853~1871

Jessie Harlan
1875~1948

M. 1897   Warren Beckwith

Mary Lincoln Beckwith "Peggy"
1898~1975

Robert Todd Lincoln Beckwith
1904~1985

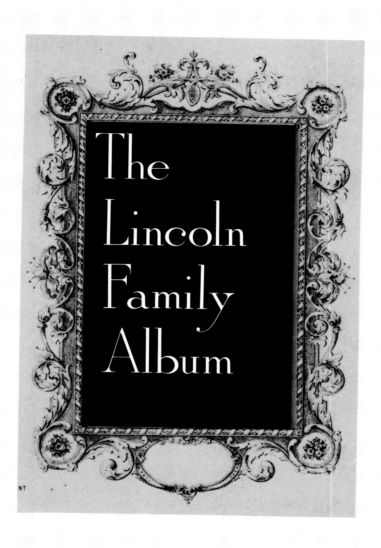

The
Lincoln
Family
Album

The Lincoln Family Album

Mark E. Neely, Jr.
& Harold Holzer

DOUBLEDAY
New York·London Toronto Sydney Auckland

For
Frank J. Williams,
friend of the family

PUBLISHED BY DOUBLEDAY
a division of Bantam Doubleday Dell Publishing Group, Inc.
666 Fifth Avenue, New York, New York 10103

DOUBLEDAY and the portrayal of an anchor
with a dolphin are trademarks of Doubleday,
a division of Bantam Doubleday Dell Publishing Group, Inc.

Library of Congress Cataloging-in-Publication Data

Neely, Mark E.
    The Lincoln family album / by Mark E. Neely, Jr., and Harold
Holzer. — 1st ed.
      p.   cm.
    1. Lincoln family—Portraits. 2. Lincoln, Abraham, 1809–1865—
Family—Portraits. I. Holzer, Harold. II. Title.
E457.25.L55N45   1990
973.7'092—dc20   89-25731
                                               CIP

ISBN 0-385-26372-4
Copyright © 1990 by Mark E. Neely, Jr. and Harold Holzer
Illustrations copyright © 1990 by The Louis A. Warren Lincoln Library
and Museum, Fort Wayne, Indiana

ACKNOWLEDGMENTS

e are indebted to the following people who generously gave advice and assistance.

We thank James T. Hickey, former curator of the Lincoln Collection at the Illinois State Historical Library, who played the principal role in rescuing and preserving the family album.

Thomas Schwartz, Jim's able successor at the Library, supplied answers to numerous questions requiring time-consuming research. Frank J. Williams, president of the Abraham Lincoln Association, provided his usual invaluable encouragement and insights.

Pamela Ross, associate librarian of Iowa Wesleyan College, and Albert C. Jerman, curator of Robert Todd Lincoln's Hildene, helped us locate information about Robert and his children.

Rex Scouten, curator of the White House, and Colonel Robert W. Hampton, director of administration for the U.S. Soldiers' and Airmen's Home, provided first-hand glimpses into family life in the Lincolns' two presidential residences in Civil War Washington. Lincoln picture historian Lloyd Ostendorf graciously provided from his collection a photograph of sculptress Vinnie Ream. And Barbara McMillan, Librarian at Mount Vernon, pointed the way to little-known recollections of Mary Lincoln's visit to George Washington's estate.

We are particularly grateful to the Lincoln National Life Insurance Company of Fort Wayne, its president, Ian M. Rolland, and senior vice-president, David D. Allen, for providing the means to acquire the collection and for funding the reproduction of all the photographs for this book.

Yvonne White and Carol Wright shepherded the paper trail between coauthors who work in Fort Wayne and New York. Both Sylvia Neely and Edith Holzer read and commented on the manuscript.

Finally, we are particularly grateful to John Duff, director of Special Interest Publishing at Doubleday, who breathed life into this project, and to Judith Daniels, former editor of *Life* magazine, who published the first preview of the collection in July 1987.

INTRODUCTION

When Abraham Lincoln, his wife Mary, and their three sons arrived in Washington for the presidential inauguration in 1861, a number of excited relatives descended on the city with them, including Mary's cousin Elizabeth Todd Grimsley. Here, they eagerly visited, among other half-finished wonders, the Washington Monument, then only a truncated stone shank surrounded by builders' debris and rubbish. In those unpolished surroundings "Lizzie" Grimsley discovered that "an enterprising photographer" had set up a makeshift studio and was taking perhaps Washington's "first carte de visites"— little photographs the size of calling cards. And with their introduction, Mrs. Grimsley noted, "the photograph album came into vogue."[1]

Abraham Lincoln and popular photography were introduced to the American people at the same time, and so too were the photo albums whose modern counterparts we take for granted today. Before 1860 photographs, which were often made of glass, were so bulky and fragile that they had to be individually packaged in hard composition cases. Since their owners could not possibly gather such photos in albums, they displayed them individually by unfastening their cases and standing them up like small open books on mantels or tables. Difficult to make and nearly impossible to copy, these photographs became prized family possessions, their subjects especially precious.

The carte de visite, which, according to an 1861 issue of the *American Journal of Photography,* "swept everything before it," caused a small parlor revolution.[2] This paper photographic print was about two inches by four inches in size, and, backed with stiff card, it could be slipped into the empty windows framed by the thick cardboard pages of a parlor album. At least a dozen patents were recorded for such albums during the Civil War, when they became essential instruments for maintaining emotional connections among families increasingly divided by the Rebellion. When family or friends called or when someone wanted to reminisce quietly about relatives in distant places or husbands and sons on battlefields, their pages provided convenient and orderly access to photographs.

Strangely, it never occurred to historians that the Lincolns themselves might have kept such an album. But they did, and later family members preserved it, adding their own portraits and snapshots to the trove. Until the last direct descendant of the sixteenth President, Robert Todd Lincoln Beckwith, died on Christmas Eve 1985, no one outside the family dreamed that such an archive had ever existed, much less survived.

While pictorial biographies of the Lincolns have appeared over the years, most featured the same handful of pictures of the President's children and descendants, many of them published originally during the Civil War and familiar in book and magazine illustrations ever since. The bulk of the family's collection, perhaps four hundred pictures altogether, remained hidden from public view. We call the whole collection the "Lincoln Family Album," though Abraham and Mary's album was but a part of it.

One of the few clues to the collection's existence had

come earlier this century from Robert Lincoln, Abraham's sole surviving son. Always generous to historians who wrote about his father, Robert occasionally loaned family pictures for copying or gave away prints of which he had extra copies. In the 1920s, for example, he sent a copy of his favorite photograph of his father to the fledgling Lincoln National Life Insurance Company in Fort Wayne, Indiana, to use as a corporate emblem.

Otherwise, Robert, who was obsessed with privacy, guarded the personal pictures of his parents, brothers, children, and himself with the same determination with which he protected his father's personal papers. And Robert's reclusive heirs followed suit, even while adding their own family pictures to the expanding collection. Long after the Abraham Lincoln papers were opened to the nation in 1947, the photographs remained in family hands, untapped and unknown.

Only in 1985, when the last of the family line, Abraham Lincoln's great-grandson Robert Beckwith, lay dying in a Virginia nursing home—an all but unknown figure who for decades successfully shunned publicity—did the existence of the family album finally come to light. By then it contained much more than the distinctive cartes of the Civil War era that Abraham and Mary Lincoln gathered in the White House. Robert Lincoln kept had his own album at Harvard, filling it with cartes of campus landmarks, famous actresses, and favorite professors. His brother Tad was once presented an album showing all the members of Company K, 150th Pennsylvania Volunteer Infantry, a unit that for a time guarded the presidential mansion. And Lincoln himself was given a copy of *The Royal Album,* a collection of photographs of the Prince of Wales and his suite, taken during his American tour in 1860; someone, probably Tad, penciled in the letter "L" under a number of the images. Robert's future wife also had albums of her own, filled with religious pictures and portraits of European royalty, family, and friends. Finally, Robert's future father-in-law, Senator James Harlan, put together an extraor-

dinary album of autographed cartes of every member who served with him in the Senate in 1864; he donated it for war relief and then bought it back. All these albums, too, were handed down to later generations of Lincolns.[3] Dozens of gilt-edged postwar studio poses as well as family snapshots were amassed by later generations of Lincolns, and the collection eventually filled an entire trunk and spilled over into drawers and closets.

Astonishingly, here were not only these later-era prints, but also some hitherto unknown examples of the primitive photographic processes that had been popular in America before paper prints and photo albums were introduced. The few pictures the Lincolns took with them from Springfield, Illinois, to Washington included several early ambrotypes of their children: milky-looking images developed directly on glass and mounted in little leather or thermoplastic cases. These portraits, too, though extremely fragile, were passed from one generation to another and saved.

By the 1860s photography had finally been freed from the one-copy-only constraints of the ambrotype and its sister processes, the daguerreotype and tintype. A Frenchman named Adolphe Eugène Disdéri perfected a multiple-lens camera capable of exposing four or more small images simultaneously on a single glass plate. From this negative, paper prints could be produced in limitless quantities, with each affixed to a small, visiting card-sized mount. The result was the carte de visite. They could be ordered four for a dollar and exchanged with family and friends. They took America by storm. "Card photographs . . . are now in the height of fashion," one observer noted. "In several of the leading galleries it makes the chief business, and in one so great is the demand that the actual work is at least a week behind the orders."[4]

Now that photographs were not only cheaper but easier to store, their uses changed. Cartes did not have to be displayed in sanctified places in the home for all to see; their subject matter need no longer be confined to idolized and

adored family members. They could now embrace subjects one was merely curious about. Soon the galleries tapped this new source of trade: the celebrity photograph. Politicians, writers, religious leaders, military heroes, and actors were invited to sit before the new carte cameras. The resulting portraits were mass-produced and sold to a public hungry for images of its political and cultural heroes, and eager to display them alongside those of friends and relatives in the new family photograph albums. By war's end, one New York City firm was offering for sale cartes of 5,000 "eminent Americans": 550 statesmen, 300 generals, 125 authors, 130 "divines," and 50 "prominent women," among others, all at $1.80 per dozen—plus albums to display them in, at 50¢ to $50 each.[5]

Today, the idea of gracing a family album with formal poses of George and Barbara Bush, James Baker, or Michael Dukakis seems ludicrous. But the dawn of the fashion for cartes de visite coincided with an era of unparalleled interest in politics and politicians. Proof of this passion can still be found in unaltered surviving family albums of ordinary nineteenth-century Americans. More often than not, their opening pages are reserved for cartes of Abraham Lincoln and other notables of the day, inserted *before* pictures of the owners' sons, daughters, and other relatives were added.

The Lincolns themselves built up their album in this conventional way. It is possible that they started early, perhaps before they left Springfield for Washington in February 1861. Visiting the Lincoln home around that time, prominent Republican Carl Schurz noticed what he thought was a family "photograph album" the size of a large Bible resting on the "customary little table with a white marble top" in the center of the parlor.[6] Even if Schurz was right and the President-elect acquired the album before moving into the White House, it would nonetheless come to be filled mainly with pictures from the family's days in Washington.

Their principal photo album, a handsome French-made volume with marbled flyleaves, featured an ornate green leather cover ringed with tacked-in brass clasps and embossed with

General Tom Thumb and Wife.

the President's initials in gold. The twenty-four thick card-board leaves had gilt edges; each leaf boasted four windows to insert cartes de visite back to back—up to 192 pictures in all. Although the little photographs themselves were removed years ago, many of the margins still bear the identifications penciled-in generations ago by Robert Lincoln.

Robert's careful identifications show that the Lincolns, like other Americans of the day, devoted the first pages of their album, fourteen in all, to celebrities: Cabinet ministers, generals, soldiers, even a Shakespearean actor. Only when their supply of such cartes was exhausted did they begin inserting pictures of their children and other relatives. Unfortunately, the final sixteen pages of the book lack identifying descriptions. We cannot know for sure what cartes they contained, if any, but we may surmise that they probably housed some of the additional pictures found loose when the Lincoln collection was discovered a century later. Like many families, the Lincolns began their photo album project with zeal, but probably ran out of energy and inspiration with the passage of time. Some readers of this book will no doubt be reminded of the albums in their own closets, with pictures from the early parts of their lives neatly placed and labeled, but pictures more recently made sitting loose in a jumble, yet to be inserted in their book and identified for posterity.

The Lincolns were not the only famous people of their time who collected pictures. Secretary of State William H. Seward, for one, whose photograph claimed the honored second place in the Lincoln album, put together several albums of his own and included in them pictures of both Abraham and Mary Lincoln. Across the Atlantic, a similar collection was being amassed by Queen Victoria, who reserved several evenings a week for "the placing [of] any new . . . photographs into the various albums," choosing her pictures with a taste more eclectic than the Lincolns', gathering cartes of deposed rulers, anonymous soldiers, places she visited, famous musicians, even subjects who had lived to the age of one hundred. "It was *such* an amusement—such an interest," declared the Queen.[7]

With similarly haphazard enthusiasm, the Lincolns set about filling their family album in the exciting days of spring 1861. The pages emphasized the military guardians of wartime Washington, government officials, political allies, and, of course, their sons. They added a photograph of Mrs. Grimsley, the Todd cousin who kept Mary company for the first six months of Lincoln's term. Like the Lincoln children, she sat for a Washington photographer, perhaps the very one she noticed near the Washington Monument, and gave her carte to Mary for the family collection. Before long, Mary's portrait album swelled with pictures of her husband's government colleagues, celebrities, friends, and family—visual souvenirs of the early days of the Administration. But when their eleven-year-old son Willie died in 1862, Mary's zeal for collecting apparently faded. For the rest of the Lincolns' White House days hardly any pictures were added. The album no longer reflected either the excitement of the present or the expectations for the future—only the irretrievable happiness of the recent past.

Mary Lincoln probably took the precious album with her when, weeks after her husband's assassination in 1865, she finally summoned the strength to rise from her sickbed and leave the White House. Perhaps it was packed in one of the crates that so overflowed with family belongings that her critics spread a rumor that Mary was stealing White House property. Surely she took it to Chicago that summer, and perhaps from there to Europe, where she lived for much of the late 1860s. When she died in a darkened room in 1882, in the same Springfield house in which, nearly forty years before, she had married Abraham Lincoln, the album was still part of her vast store of property. From Mary it passed to Robert; from Robert, to his children and grandchildren.

These pictures, together with those accumulated later by Robert and his descendants, have now come to the Louis A. Warren Lincoln Library and Museum, the very collection founded by Lincoln National Life in 1928 as a gesture of thanks to Robert Lincoln for lending the family name, as well as a single photograph of his father, to the young insurance firm.

On the pages that follow, the first attempt is made to present a selective chronology of important pictures from each generation: not only photographs from the albums themselves, but also the early ambrotypes from the Springfield years, as well as the post–Civil War portraits and snaphots of Robert and his progeny. Reproducing all the images in the collection would be neither possible nor very illuminating, because the Lincolns owned many poses now quite familiar to Civil War enthusiasts.

This book instead emphasizes pictures that the public has rarely seen before; most have never appeared in any book. The order in which we present them, it should be noted, is our own, not the Lincolns'. We offer them chronologically, with Springfield faces first, then the White House collection, and finally the pictures of the descendants. Taken together, this sampling from the collection significantly multiplies the previously known photographs of the Lincoln family, and with them our previously attained knowledge about the family itself. It expands our understanding of the Lincolns' White House years, and it reveals for the first time the sad story of the descendants shaped by their tragic family history.

The Lincoln family album illustrates intimately all those generational threads—the warp and woof of family fabric. The Lincoln family history has been amply documented. But it has never been seen—until now.

AUTHORS' NOTE ON FAMILY NAMES AND FAMILY PICTURES

History remembers her as Mary Todd Lincoln, but the President's wife never referred to herself as such after her marriage. She was always Mary Lincoln, Mrs. A. Lincoln, or Mrs. Abraham Lincoln. On the pages that follow, we try to follow suit, that is, until the arrival into the family of son Robert Lincoln's bride, whose name was also Mary, and the birth of their first child, Mary yet again. For the next thirteen years there were three living Mary Lincolns. To avoid confusion, then, we begin referring to them—in captions to pictures made between 1868 and 1882—as Mary Todd Lincoln, Mary Harlan Lincoln, and Mary Lincoln (the last-named, whenever possible, as Mamie, her nickname).

A fourth Mary, a great-granddaughter, would arrive near the end of the century. A second Abraham Lincoln, the President's grandson, mercifully called himself Jack, some claimed out of reverence for the hallowed name he inherited.

Similarly, biographers have usually referred to Lincoln's sole surviving son as Robert Todd Lincoln, but here again, they did not follow Robert's own preference. He never used his mother's maiden name. He called himself Robert T. Lincoln or R. T. Lincoln, and we have done the same. Strangely, his own grandson would be given all the family names: the last of the Lincolns was named Robert Todd Lincoln Beckwith.

As noted earlier, all the Lincoln children, grandchildren, and great-grandchildren are represented in this book, along with a healthy sampling of the celebrity pictures Mary Lincoln collected in the White House. Space constraints made it impossible to include all of them, but it is probably useful to know some of those that have been omitted. First, a number of cartes de visite of Willie and Tad that have appeared in previous books have been left out to make room for hitherto unpublished portraits. We have included some of the souvenir scenic views Mary Lincoln collected, but have left out others, including pictures of the Smithsonian Institution, the War Department, and Washington's City Hall. There were pictures of both generals and governors that we did not use. The album also included cartes of most members of the Lincoln Cabinet; we have included but a representative two. We mention the other pictures to provide the most thorough possible view of Mary's collecting proclivities, even though there is not room to present all of the photographs.

Among the photographs of Abraham Lincoln, we present only the pictures we strongly suspect or know for sure the family chose to save. In addition, Robert had new prints made of his favorite pictures of his father over the years and retained other undistinguished copies sent to him by admirers. We have made an effort to winnow out the genuinely important pieces, a task to which we brought a rigid rationale based in part on Abraham Lincoln's apparent reluctance to pose and lack of interest in the copies that resulted from his occasional sittings. Asked for a photograph of himself shortly before the Republican National Convention that nominated him for President in 1860, Lincoln replied, "I have not a single one now at my control."[8] Fortunately, his family retained control of enough portraits—as well as pictures of their relatives and descendants—to make the family album complete.

THE GILDED PRISON

> Happy families are all alike;
> every unhappy family
> is unhappy in its own way.
>
> —*Leo Tolstoy*

To the modern reader this will probably seem like the album of an unhappy family. By and large, it is. And the technical constraints of primitive photography make it seem even more so. The Lincolns' White House album contains no pictures of the baby's christening, of presents eagerly opened on Christmas morning, or of the Fourth of July picnic in the park. But such subjects will not be found in any other album from those early days of photography. Before the invention of flexible film and the advent of portable cameras in the 1880s, snapshots were beyond the abilities of photographic technology. In the Civil War era, photographs were produced by coating a stiff plate with sticky chemicals and developing the image immediately. The cameraman needed abundant light and cooperative sitters, for lens exposures were lengthy. Subjects who were likely to move suddenly and violently were seldom attempted. Wriggling babies, therefore, were not usually taken to the skylighted studios, though dead ones were sometimes photographed to keep the survivors' memories fresh. The Lincolns did own a couple of rather unusual pictures of their pets: Fido, a dog left behind in Springfield when they moved to Washington, and the

youngest boy's South American pony, a gift while the Lincolns resided in the White House. The picture of the squirming dog, not surprisingly, is blurred.

For the most part, the photographs that belonged to Abraham and Mary Lincoln consisted of rigid portraits posed inside studios in Illinois and Washington. The solemnity of the era, when proper people were enjoined to be earnest and not pleasure-seeking, conspired with the sluggish camera shutter to reveal a world populated for the most part with stern sobersides. Abraham Lincoln had a wonderful sense of humor, and his wife was given to witty and sparkling conversation. They likely enjoyed the company of similar people, especially before family tragedies and national political disasters cast a pall over their lives. But little humor can be detected in the Lincoln family album. In fact, Mrs. Lincoln did not like to be photographed in part for the very reason that the results made her look too stern.

Whatever the limitations of nineteenth-century photographic technology, the tragic Lincoln family was destined to gather pictures from a sad life. The presidency destroyed the Lincoln family circle. The consequences were perhaps predictable even before the Lincolns moved to Washington. On October 20, 1860, Mary told a friend, "This summer, we have had . . . no time to be occupied, with home affairs." She referred, of course, to the summer of the presidential election campaign. The customs of campaigning for the presidency were different then, and it was thought improper for a presidential candidate to travel or speak in his own behalf. Lincoln did not give a single speech or leave Springfield to go on the hustings in the summer of 1860, but a steady stream of visitors on political business came to see him. There was "no time" for "home affairs."[1]

And no more time for home ever came to them again. Not until 1864 did Lincoln order a door installed between his office and the family apartments; only then could he enjoy direct access to the private rooms of the White House without threading his way through groups of visitors in the halls. In 1865 Mary said of her marriage, "Notwithstanding our opposite natures, our lives have been eminently peaceful." But it had been "peaceful" in Washington mostly by dint of radical separation of their spheres. "We are surrounded, at all times, by a great deal of company," Mrs. Lincoln wistfully pointed out around election time in 1864. Mary traveled widely, and the President worked hard when she was at home. "I consider myself fortunate, if at eleven o'clock, I once more find myself, in my pleasant room & very especially, if my tired & weary Husband, is *there,* resting in the lounge to receive me—to chat over the occurrences of the day."[2]

Mary admitted, after her husband's death, that on their last carriage excursion together, on the very afternoon before their fateful visit to Ford's Theatre, he had said, reflecting on their lives in the White House, "we have both, been very miserable." Mrs. Lincoln revealed this at a time in her life when she idealized her marriage more than ever. Considering its source and setting, it is a stunning revelation. Yet Mrs. Lincoln's candor has failed to persuade twentieth-century authors, many of whom sentimentalize the Lincoln marriage and routinely underestimate the destructive impact of the presidency on family life.[3]

From 1858 on, the family was rarely together. Lincoln campaigned vigorously for the fledgling Republican Party from 1858 to 1860. His oldest son, Robert, after failing the entrance examination for Harvard, was packed off to preparatory school at Exeter in New Hampshire for the 1859–60 year, and in his mother's overdramatic assessment of Lincoln family life in his absence, "light & mirth . . . departed with him." He matriculated at Harvard after that and "never unpacked his trunk at the White House." Whenever he mentioned the separation after 1865, Robert stressed the distance he felt from the White House and his famous father. "He came to Washington for short visits during his vacations, but he did not regard the White House as his home," reported an article on Robert in "Celebrities at Home," published in the 1880s. Robert graduated from college in 1864 and enrolled in law school, but a few months later

he joined General Ulysses S. Grant's staff in Virginia.[4]

The White House was home for William Wallace Lincoln, the Lincolns' promising third son, for less than a year before the child died. After February 1862 only Mary, Tad, and Abraham resided there regularly, thoughts of the heartbreaking loss of Willie frequently on their minds. As Mary described the family tragedy, "the *serpents*" had "crossed our pathways."[5]

For a brief and shining interval, however, while Willie was still alive, Mary Lincoln enthusiastically assembled the photographic mementos of an exciting life. Happiest of all, understandably, were the days that fell in the brief span between Lincoln's election in November 1860 and the fall of Fort Sumter in mid-April 1861, which ignited the Civil War. Lincoln's victory came as a great relief to his wife, who confessed two weeks before election day, "I scarcely know, how I would bear up, under defeat." She did not have to in the end, and adjusting to victory at first proved easy. "I am beginning to feel so perfectly at home, and enjoy every thing so much," Mary wrote, after about three weeks in the White House. What she liked best about it, though, was that it was not at all like home in Springfield. "Every evening," she now boasted, "our *blue room,* is filled with the elite of the land, last eve, we had about 40 to call in, to see us *ladies,* from Vice P. Breckinridge down." Mrs. Lincoln adapted quickly to Washington's hierarchical society, arranged in a great pyramid descending from the President to the Vice President and on "down" the social ladder.[6]

Mr. and Mrs. Lincoln were not alike in their anxieties over social status. More characteristic of Abraham was his brief speech to an Ohio regiment, on August 22, 1864: "I happen temporarily to occupy this big White House. I am a living witness that any one of your children may look to come here as my father's child has." Mary had a different outlook. Long after she departed the White House, she still looked down on "the very *middle classes*" and told her daughter-in-law, "I do not consider ourselves in that category."[7]

The Lincoln album was more the pretentious Mary's than

the egalitarian Abraham's. It contains as many likenesses of princes and European diplomats as frontier politicians. And one searches altogether in vain for photographs of Lincoln's rustic relatives, such as his cousins Dennis and John Hanks, both of whom had posed for readily available portraits. Todd relatives, on the other hand, were well represented between the album's thick green leather covers.

The Todd emphasis mirrored the reality of the Lincolns' life, for when Abraham Lincoln married Mary Todd, he divorced his family for hers. This was especially apparent when he was elected President and hungry Todd relatives gathered in Washington for the division of the political loaves and fishes. In the early days of the Administration, the White House was filled with Mary's family, and her obscure relatives are disproportionately represented in the album she started at that time.

Abraham Lincoln was not only able but virtually obligated to reward his loyal political friends in the era before civil service reform. He could also hand out offices to his relatives, as almost all politicians in the era did. Every member of Lincoln's Cabinet obtained a job in the government or a military promotion for a member of his family. Secretary of State William H. Seward, for example, provided for his three sons by making Frederick the assistant secretary of state, Augustus an army paymaster, and William H. Seward, Jr., a lieutenant colonel.[8] Lincoln made the same sorts of appointments, but he did show some sensitivity to appearances and did not favor his own blood relatives.

His wife's family, on the other hand, were bountifully provided with jobs—despite their tendency to vote for the opposition Democrats. Mary's older sister Elizabeth was married to a Springfield lawyer and politician named Ninian Wirt Edwards. Though by 1860 he was a confirmed Democrat, Edwards received an appointment from Lincoln as a captain and commissary of subsistence on August 8, 1861. William S. Wallace, who had married Mary's sister Frances, was made a major and paymaster on May 15, 1861. And the husband of

Mary's half sister Margaret, Charles C. Kellogg, gained appointment as a captain and commissary of subsistence on February 19, 1863. The three Lincoln brothers-in-law each served throughout the war in these positions. Other Todd relatives received similarly favorable treatment, including Lockwood M. Todd, Mary's cousin, who became a captain and commissary of subsistence on March 25, 1864.[9] Photographs of most of these handsomely rewarded Todds appear in the Lincoln Family Album: Elizabeth Edwards, William Wallace, Charles and Margaret Kellogg, and cousin Lockwood.

Theirs were not heroic frontline jobs with the army, and the appeal of these positions lay only partly in their capacity to tender selfless service to the nation in its hour of trial. They were also profitable. Indeed, Edwards sought office mainly because he was suffering "pecuniary embarrassment" at the time. When, after gaining his appointment, he awarded contracts to Springfield Democrat Joel Matteson, local Republicans howled with indignation and accused Edwards of profiting from his office to the tune of $15,000. He explained to Lincoln that he had indeed extricated himself from his earlier financial distress, but this was by dint of frugal household savings rather than by increasing his income by exploiting his political connections. The President expressed sober confidence in his brother-in-law, affirming on June 15, 1863, that he did "not suppose Mr. Edwards has, at this time of his life, given up his old habits, and turned dishonest." Nevertheless, Lincoln did admit that Edwards "could have saved me from this" if he cared; instead, Lincoln's old Springfield friends had been "harassing" him "for now nearly two years" and had recently renewed "the pressure" on him. Eventually, the President refused to fire Edwards but transferred him to Chicago and found a more politically acceptable replacement for him in Springfield.[10]

Other Todd relatives proved troublesome as well. Something of a ne'er-do-well, Lockwood Todd needed a political appointment to get on in the world. Born in Springfield, Lockwood lived for twelve years in California but returned home shortly before the war, and then set off with several other Todd relatives for Washington to get an office from his presidential relative. California patronage presented complicated problems for Lincoln, however; a delegation of far-western office-seekers had already visited him in Springfield, before he left for his inauguration. The best California office at Lincoln's disposal went to Ira B. Rankin, who became Collector of the Port of San Francisco. According to Lockwood Todd, Lincoln in return extracted from Rankin a promise to appoint Todd "Drayman of the Port." This rather mundane position could be quite remunerative. By employing four or five horses and wagons to carry imported goods from the port to designated government warehouses for inspection, a drayman stood to earn perhaps $2,500 a year. When Rankin realized how profitable the job could be, he seized on a golden political opportunity to cut poor Lockwood out of the deal. A petition protesting Todd's worthiness to receive the patronage job arrived at the White House from San Francisco Republicans, who pointed out that he was a Democrat who had vigorously stumped for Lincoln's rival, Stephen A. Douglas, in California in 1860. Lockwood denied an allegation that he had used abusive language about Mr. and Mrs. Lincoln in the campaign, for he had "from a boy . . . been taught by our dear father to regard Mr. Lincoln as the best and purest of men." Lockwood maintained that he was "always a favorite with both him and Mary" and that he had "been a great deal at Mr. Lincolns House, frequently staying there while he was absent at court."[11]

Nevertheless, when Rankin sent the Republicans' protest to Lincoln, the President's secretary, John G. Nicolay, replied: "That not being conversant thoroughly with the matter that he (The President) is unable to decide. And requests the Collector to act as he thinks best in the Case."[12]

In the end Lincoln gave no reply and Collector Rankin quickly made his own brother drayman. Lockwood was left out in the cold. Eventually the collector's reputation for corruption caused so many complaints to pour into the Treasury Depart-

ment that in the spring of 1863 Secretary Salmon P. Chase had to send a special agent to investigate. Rankin was removed.[13] But Todd still did not get the coveted drayage contract. He had to be content with appointment as a captain and commissary of subsistence in 1864. Though he would not represent Lincoln at the port of San Francisco, Lockwood Todd was represented in the family album.

Lockwood's brother, John Blair Smith Todd, was a public figure in his own right, and one senses a genuine respect for him in Lincoln's correspondence. He was a West Point graduate and a nineteen-year veteran of the professional army. While stationed in the Dakota Territory in 1856, he resigned from the army to become a merchant and Indian trader. A man of shrewdness and vision, Todd later played a major role in territorial organization and government. Given his connection with the new President, he might have hoped to be appointed territorial governor, but he was a Democrat too, and though party affiliation was not necessarily an insuperable obstacle to getting a lucrative but lowly appointment as drayman, it would always be a serious objection for a position as politically important as territorial governor. Lincoln awarded the coveted gubernatorial spot instead to a Springfield neighbor and Republican, Dr. William Jayne. As he was also the brother-in-law of Illinois Senator Lyman Trumbull, the appointment could be made with fewer complaints from important politicians with their own patronage hopefuls to champion.[14]

Along with other members of the Todd clan, J. B. S. Todd came to Washington for the division of the spoils but after a few weeks returned to the West via Springfield. Mary sent with him "some photographs of the boys," probably copies of the same poses shown on the following pages. Moreover, the President gave him an assignment, too. Lincoln told the Secretary of War on the eve of Todd's departure, "Capt. Todd leaves for the West to-morrow afternoon; and, being an experienced military man, would bear and deliver any dispatches confided to him." In this chaotic period in Washing-

ton, when the President still feared that the government departments and the military ranks were riddled with traitors who had not yet gone South to cast their lot with the Confederacy, Lincoln was more likely to deal with someone he knew and trusted than with unknown officials. Later, when the President was obliged to explain to an enquiring Congress how public funds were handled by the government in this crisis, he said:

> The several departments of the government at that time contained so large a number of disloyal persons that it would have been impossible to provide safely, through official agents only, for the performance of the duties . . . confided to citizens favorably known for their ability, loyalty, and patriotism.
>
> The several orders issued upon these occurrences were transmitted by private messengers, who pursued a circuitous way to the seaboard cities, inland, across the States of Pennsylvania and Ohio and the northern lakes. I believe that by these and other similar measures taken in that crisis, some of which were without any authority of law, the government was saved from overthrow.[15]

J. B. S. Todd was not only a military veteran but also a thoroughly loyal Unionist. Shortly after the firing on Fort Sumter, he became a conduit for information about the fate of Union sentiment in the crucial border state of Kentucky. William Nelson, a Kentucky Unionist, sent two letters to Todd in April, which he shared with the President. The situation in Kentucky was perilous, they said, but not hopeless.[16]

After he returned to the Dakota Territory, Todd gained election as territorial delegate to Congress in September. He also garnered an appointment from the Lincoln Administration on September 19, 1861, as a Brigadier General of Volunteers, serving in Missouri. On November 21 he tendered his resignation, to take effect on April 30. He asked for a delay pending advice on the constitutional problem raised by his election. The U.S. Constitution stipulates that "no Person

holding any Office under the United States, shall be a Member of either House during his Continuance in Office." Territorial delegates were not full voting members of Congress, and Todd thought he could perhaps maintain his military rank. Apparently he could, for he did not resign until mid-July 1862, by which time he was commanding the 6th Division of the Army Corps of the Tennessee, under Ulysses S. Grant.[17]

John Blair Smith Todd was never completely reliant on Lincoln, and his course hereafter proved quite independent. Even his military appointment was hardly a sign of dependence, for this was an appointment to field command. The Civil War was a national war, and Democrats and Republicans alike had to hold military rank for the North to win. Todd continued his adherence to the Democratic Party and gained reelection as territorial delegate. He ran against William Jayne, the Republican territorial governor in 1862, but party lines were so loose in the West that the historian of the Dakota Territory Howard R. Lamar says that the "main issue was over which of the candidates had the most influence with President Lincoln, his physician or his wife's cousin." Todd later served as speaker of the territorial house and eventually as territorial governor.[18]

The sad truth apparent in these family patronage deals is that the Administration probably got the worst of the bargain: the less able men, such as Lockwood Todd and William Wallace, received appointments. Capable men, such as J. B. S. Todd, served the Democratic Party in their own right.

For his part, President Lincoln was at least apologetic about his role as dispenser of patronage to kinsmen. Less than thirty days into his Administration, Lincoln had to write to one cousin about yet another cousin, Elizabeth Todd Grimsley, who spent the first six months of his term living in the White House and lobbying for the job of Springfield postmistress:

Cousin Lizzie shows me your letter of the 27th. The question of giving her the Springfield Post-office troubles me.

You see I have already appointed William Jayne a territorial governor, and . . . Trumbulls brother to a Land-office. Will it do for me to go on and justify the declaration that Trumbull and I have divided out all of the offices among our relatives? Dr. Wallace, you know, is needy, and looks to me; and I personally owe him much.

Despite the political risks Lincoln took to help his wife's relatives, his efforts did not always garner the gratitude that Mary, at least, expected. Mary thus complained to a correspondent about her sister Frances Wallace's ingratitude:

Notwithstanding Dr W—— has received his portion, in life, from the Administration, yet Frances always remains quiet. E[lizabeth Todd Edwards]. in her letter said—Frances often spoke of Mr L's kindness—in giving him his place. She little knows, what a hard battle, I had for it—and how near, he came getting nothing.[19]

By contrast with the Todds, Lincoln's kith and kin fared rather poorly. Of course, they were less well equipped by education and experience to hold government jobs, and even before the era of civil service reform, the President did not want anyone in his Administration so incompetent as to cause scandal. When Lincoln's deceased mother's cousin John Hanks let it be known that he desired an office, the President probably wanted to oblige this man, whom he liked and trusted. But what was Lincoln to do? Hanks, like most of his relatives, was illiterate. Even commissaries of subsistence, positions offered as sops to applicants who could not be given higher jobs in the Administration, had to meet minimum qualifications. An act of Congress passed in the summer of 1864 stipulated that "every quartermaster and assistant quartermaster, and every commissary and assistant commissary of subsistence, and every paymaster and additional paymaster shall, as soon as practicable, be ordered to appear for examination as to his qualifications before a board." The board was to conduct its examination "with impartiality, and with a sole view to the qualifications of the person or persons to be examined." The examinees had to prove they possessed "the requisite business qualifications," and proof of failure "by reason of intemperance, gambling, or other immorality" could, if the President agreed, result in dismissal from the service without pay. The business skills of most members of the not very distinguished Hanks family were probably not equal to the task.[20]

Fortunately, Mr. Lincoln did not have to worry much because, as his wife pointed out, he had few close relatives:

> . . . *he has neither brother nor sister, aunt or uncle, and only a few third cousins, no nearer ones. . . . Those whom he would have cared to see prospering, did not really require his assistance. At any rate on no terms would either male or female receive, his signature to enable them to profit by our Government.*

To Mary, whose standards in such matters were not as high, her husband seemed "a monomaniac on the subject of honesty."[21]

Abraham Lincoln did have a family of his own, of course, but there is no evidence of it in the photo album. His mother died long before the introduction of photography in America, and as far as is known, no picture was ever taken of his father, though he did not die until 1851. Poverty and their residence in remote rural areas would have conspired to keep them out of the camera's eye. Lincoln's stepmother, Sarah Bush Johnston Lincoln, was photographed once late in life, but Mary owned no copy of the portrait—not surprisingly, since Mary's relationship with her mother-in-law was quite distant. She wrote only one known letter to her (along with a follow-up note merely requesting acknowledgment of receipt of a package announced in the letter). Dated a week before Christmas 1867, the letter was dignified and correct in every way, but it was terribly formal. It also is the source of the astounding revelation that Abraham Lincoln had never provided a headstone for his penurious father's grave. In their astonishment at this, biographers have scarcely noticed Mary's own surprising statement to Mrs. Lincoln: "Perhaps you know that our youngest boy, is named for your husband, Thomas Lincoln, this child, the idol of his father." Not only had Thomas—Tad, as his parents called him—never met his grandmother, but his mother never before bothered to tell her mother-in-law that he was named for his grandfather Lincoln![22]

One hopes that, if not Mary, then perhaps Abraham had informed his beloved stepmother earlier of the family significance of the boy's Christian name—perhaps on one of Lincoln's trips to her homestead in Coles County, Illinois. Possibly Mary was only groping for some pleasant subject to discuss with her mother-in-law that might avoid the real subject inevitably on their minds: the lack of any communication between the two Mrs. Lincolns over the twenty-five years that had passed since Mary Todd married Sarah Lincoln's stepson.

For his part, though extremely fond of Sarah, as she was of him, Abraham could not have owned a photograph of her, because she was not photographed until well after his murder. Yet the absence of pictures in the album from the Lincoln side of the family makes clear the direction he had taken in his life: away from the hardscrabble world of the Lincolns toward the established comfort of the Todds. Mary accelerated that move, but the ambitious Springfield lawyer was already headed in that direction when he met her.

To be sure, Lincoln's relatives may have been slighted simply because family photograph albums were a domestic responsibility in nineteenth-century family life and therefore fell into Mary's sphere in that era of strictly segregated duties of gender. On July 26, 1862, in fact, Mrs. Lincoln told a friend, "I have just placed the carte-de-visite, of your sweet little girl, in my Album." Mary did not say "our album."[23]

No album that Mary controlled was likely to contain a photograph of one of the major critics of Lincoln's marriage, William Herndon. Though not a relative, he was Lincoln's longtime law partner. Herndon was also an ardent Republican and an intelligent man of some considerable learning, at least by Springfield standards. But Herndon always had a troubled relationship with Lincoln's wife. As Mary put it later, he was not a "habitué" of the Lincoln home. Herndon was unwelcome there; the office was more in his line. Herndon knew his place and never really pressed his old partner for a federal job. When he did ask help for his fiancée's brother-in-law, Lincoln found employment for him, but Herndon himself never served the Lincoln Administration. The President did once offer him a poor-paying claims commission job; Herndon was needy but turned it down. In later years he remembered the pain of this circumstance with an observation that was probably half-accurate: "Lincoln was a selfish man generally and especially in the political world but was blindly generous to his *own*." It is not surprising that there is no picture of Herndon in the album. If there ever had been, it would surely have been excised by Mary in 1866, when Herndon's lectures on a supposed early romance between Lincoln and a New Salem girl named Ann Rutledge made the President's marriage seem loveless.[24]

Except for family relations, Mrs. Lincoln had little appreciable political influence on her husband. While he was stumping for presidential candidate John C. Frémont and the Republican ticket back in 1856, she was complaining in a bigoted way about the "wild Irish" and shallowly expressing sympathy for the anti-Catholic third-party presidential candidate, Millard Fillmore.[25] Though she developed interest in black emancipation in the White House years, as late as 1860 she spoke enviously of a cousin who lived "in a very handsome house, four stories, plenty of room & some Kentucky *darkies*, to wait on them." Mrs. Lincoln was often a poor judge of character and surrounded herself with a hardly trustworthy coterie in the White House. Some of these persons went on to embarrass Lincoln politically, as did Mary's own thoughtless extravagance in exceeding a generous congressional appropriation to redecorate the executive mansion.[26]

Nonetheless, before the war years brought embarrassment and tragedy, Mrs. Lincoln relished the trappings of political success. "One day this week," she wrote on March 28, "we went down to Mt Vernon." The President, preoccupied by the Sumter crisis and busy staffing his new Administration, did not join her for the trip aboard the steamer *Thomas Collyer*. Surely he must have wanted to, for George Washington was often on his mind during this trying period. The great patriot's image had grown larger and larger for most Americans as the sectional crisis deepened. The popular movement to save Washington's home was a product of the same times that launched Abraham Lincoln into the White House. From 1856 to 1860 the Mount Vernon Ladies' Association of the Union waged a campaign to save the historic house, after Congress had spurned appeals to purchase it for the nation. The Massachusetts orator and politician Edward Everett, who in 1863 would join Lincoln on the speaker's platform at Gettysburg, had recently prepared an oration on "The Character of Washington." He devised the idea of repeating the speech throughout the Union to raise funds for the Mount Vernon preservation project, and went on to deliver it 129 times, raising half the required money single-handedly.[27]

The point of Everett's much admired address may have moved many donors to help save the house on the Potomac:

But to us citizens of America, it belongs above all others to show respect to the memory of Washington, by the practical deference which we pay to those sober maxims of public policy which he has left us,—a last testament of affection in his Farewell Address. Of all the exhortations which it contains, I scarce need say to you that none are so emphatically uttered, none so anxiously repeated, as those which enjoin the preservation of the Union of these States. On this, under Providence, it depends in the judgment of Washington whether the people of America shall follow the Old World example, and be broken up into a group of independent military powers, wasted by eternal border wars, feeding the ambition of petty sovereigns on the life-blood of wasted principalities,—a custom-house on the bank of every river, a fortress on every frontier hill, a pirate lurking in the recesses of every bay,—or whether they shall continue to constitute a confederate republic, the most extensive, the most powerful, the most prosperous in the long line of ages. No one can read the Farewell Address without feeling that this was the thought and this the care which lay nearest and heaviest upon that noble heart; and if—which Heaven forbid—the day shall ever arrive when his parting counsels on that head shall be forgotten, on that day, come it soon or come it late, it may as mournfully as truly be said, that Washington has lived in vain. Then the vessels as they ascend and descend the Potomac may toll their bells with new significance as they pass Mount Vernon; they will strike the requiem of constitutional liberty for us,—for all nations.

As historian George B. Forgie later put it, saving Mount Vernon became a symbol for saving the Union—to Everett, anyway (its "Ladies" were in fact Southerners, and doubtless later went along with secession, though Mount Vernon itself was by agreement specifically exempted from destruction by either side in the war).

The Lincolns never openly expressed the customary romantic "associations" upon visiting the place—the subject of a contemporary book by Benson J. Lossing, *Mount Vernon and Its Associations*. With half sister Margaret in tow, Mrs. Lincoln arrived, just "like *anybody* else" in the admiring words of Mount Vernon's resident secretary. The weather was "Marchy and disagreeable," but Mary gamely toured the house and grounds and sat down to a simple meal of bread, butter, and ham.[28] Mary said nothing at all of feelings evoked by seeing Washington's home, but she did obtain photographs of it for her album. As for Abraham, who mentioned George Washington several times in his speeches, he was not much given to romantic sentiments of place. When Mrs. Lincoln repeated her excursion to Washington's home in 1862, Mr. Lincoln traveled with the party but stayed on board the boat while the rest of the group went ashore to see the house.

Lincoln was rarely moved by visual arts, natural wonders, or historic sites. He is not known to have commented on the statue of Andrew Jackson that he could see from the White House windows every day, though Mary placed a carte of the sculpture in the family album, among the other familiar scenes of Washington she obtained. Yet Lincoln had thought much about Andrew Jackson in his life, and the old general was especially on his mind in Lincoln's first days in Washington in 1861. Jackson was a Democrat, but even so, Lincoln evinced a grudging admiration for him. He never allowed partisan opposition to Jackson's political principles to diminish his appreciation for the general's great military victory over the British at New Orleans in the War of 1812. And he once admonished his own party, which championed legislative powers more than executive, for ignoring one secret of Jackson's popularity: his willingness to take responsibility and act alone, an example Lincoln would follow with his Emancipation Proclamation. When Lincoln was faced with the need to state his policy on secession in his first inaugural address, he consulted only four documents: the Constitution, Henry Clay's speech on the compromise of 1850, Daniel Webster's second reply to Hayne, and Jackson's proclamation against Nullification. Later, when war broke out and pro-slavery forces in Maryland complained about federal troops marching across their soil to protect the nation's capital, Lincoln exploded in a rare fit of public anger: "You would have me break my oath and surrender the Government without a blow. There is no Washington in that—no Jackson in that—no manhood nor honor in that." Lincoln felt strongly about Jackson, but art failed to evoke a response. Words were the way to Lincoln's heart. Pictures never much inspired him, so he took no apparent interest in the family photo album.[29]

Profound "associations" never were in Mary's line; she preferred the shimmering superficial world of society and fashion. She did, however, retain deep feelings about intimate family life. No one could outdo Mary in maternal affection, and the plight of unhappy children anywhere genuinely touched her, even nameless waifs suffering in the streets. She was also well read, as women of her station and period went, and the sort of literature that deeply moved her was that written by Charles Dickens. "Dickens told many truths, in his school narrations," Mary said, when she saw how poor Tad's fare was when he boarded in an English school in 1870. Boarding schools always unnerved her, since she knew their lonely hardships firsthand. When she looked one over for Tad in Wisconsin, in 1867, she reported: "My feelings were especially *moved,* by seeing the little white cots of the boys, where they are wont, to repose so far away, from the loving Mothers, who would at any moment, give almost their life to see them." There "was an air of *restraint*" at the school which Mrs. Lincoln "did not exactly like," even though she recognized "the necessity" for the undisciplined and embarrassingly ill-educated Tad to be "taught obedience by kind & gentle school treatment." Even back in 1860, she had read with unusual interest a book her husband brought home from a political trip to New York, pressed on him, no doubt, by an earnest founder of the Five Points House of Industry, a school for poor children. She apparently recommended *The Lost and Found; or Life among the Poor,* a volume about maltreated children by Samuel Byram Halliday, to some of her friends in Springfield.[30]

Mrs. Lincoln was not worrying about Tad's education in the spring of 1861. She continued to enjoy herself even after war began. The contrast between the moods of the Lincolns at this time was sharp. Later she recalled the White House period before February 1862 as *"so much bliss."* Yet it was anything but blissful for her husband. In fact, it probably was the worst period of his Administration and perhaps the worst period of his life since the 1840s.[31]

It began with the fall of Fort Sumter in April 1861. Massachusetts troops rushed south to protect the capital. When a mob in Baltimore blocked their way, a bloody riot ensued. Then the railroad bridges in Baltimore were burned, and Washington was for a time completely isolated from the North. Enterprising railroad executives rigged a route to

Washington that avoided Baltimore, but troops did not reach the capital immediately. Washington assumed the posture of a besieged city, and the government grew anxious. The President's admiring private secretaries, John G. Nicolay and John Hay, who were also represented in the Lincoln family album, described those tense days in the White House this way:

. . . Lincoln, almost a giant in physical stature and strength, combined in his intellectual nature a masculine courage and power of logic with an ideal sensitiveness of conscience and a sentimental tenderness as delicate as a woman's. This Presidential trust which he had assumed was to him not a mere regalia of rank and honor. Its terrible duties and responsibilities seemed rather a coat of steel armor, heavy to bear, and cutting remorselessly into the quick flesh. That one of the successors of Washington should find himself even to this degree in the hands of his enemies was personally humiliating; but that the majesty of a great nation should be thus insulted and its visible symbols of authority be placed in jeopardy; above all, that the hitherto glorious example of the republic to other nations should stand in this peril of surprise and possible sudden collapse, the Constitution be scoffed, and human freedom become a by-word and reproach—this must have begot in him an anxiety approaching torture.

In the eyes of his countrymen and of the world he was holding the scales of national destiny; he alone knew that for the moment the forces which made the beam vibrate with such uncertainty were beyond his control. In others' society he gave no sign of these inner emotions. But once, on the afternoon of the 23rd, the business of the day being over, the Executive office deserted, after walking the floor alone in silent thought for nearly half an hour, he stopped and gazed long and wistfully out of the window down the Potomac in the direction of the expected ships; and, unconscious of other presence in the room, at length broke out with irrespressible anguish in the repeated exclamation, "Why don't they come! Why don't they come!"

Of course, Mrs. Lincoln felt the danger too, commenting two days after relief arrived, "Thousands of soldiers are guarding us, and if there is safety in numbers, we have every reason, to feel secure. We can only hope for peace!" By July, she could assure a friend in Illinois, apprehensive about paying a visit to the capital, that "there is no place in the country, so safe & well guarded as Washington." She was no doubt pleased to insert photos of some of the city's defenders in her album: General Winfield Scott, General Cassius M. Clay, a Captain Henry B. Todd (no relation), and Colonel Elmer E. Ellsworth.[32]

With security came a return to social excitement in the executive mansion, and with that, concern over its shabby appearance. The difference in outlook between husband and wife was never more sharply delineated than in the near scandal of redecorating the White House. Mrs. Lincoln overspent a generous congressional appropriation, and when Mr. Lincoln learned of it—not from Mary herself, significantly—he grew furious, saying that "it would stink in the nostrils of the American people to have it said that the President of the United States had approved a bill overrunning an appropriation of $20,000 for *flub dubs,* for this damned old house, when the soldiers cannot have blankets." Lincoln was exactly right about how the opposition press would regard his wife's callous extravagance. Besides, as he pointed out, the White House was "better than any one we ever lived in."[33]

This episode, which occurred in December 1861, revealed the strain the presidency was exerting on the Lincoln family. Mrs. Lincoln was feeling at "home" in what Mr. Lincoln regarded as "this damned old house." Most evident was the increasing distance between husband and wife: she put the commissioner of public buildings up to seeing the President to explain the cost overruns, asking the commissioner not to tell her husband she had spoken to him.

True, the Lincolns enjoyed new creature comforts in Washington unlike any they were used to in Springfield, but these by no means ensured happiness or family closeness. As Mrs. Lincoln pointed out to a friend, the situation was "very different *from home.*" The days of cooking and cleaning were past. "We only have to give our orders for the dinner," she boasted, "and *dress* in proper season." On another occasion, she said, with hauteur exaggerated for humorous effect, "we have only *three* carriages, at our command." Servants were numerous, including a steward, William Slade; a cook, Cornelia Mitchell; and a butler and waiter, Peter Brown.[34] There are no photographs in the family album of these servants with whom the Lincolns had daily association for years.

If class distinctions were more clearly defined in Lincoln's day than many modern Americans imagine, racial lines were even more strictly drawn. All of these servants were black, as was Mrs. Lincoln's famous seamstress, Elizabeth Keckley, with whom she was for a time reputedly very close. Mrs. Keckley's likeness cannot be found in the album, either, but Mrs. Lincoln had a falling out with her after the war, when her seamstress wrote a "behind the scenes" memoir and without permission published some of Mary's letters to her. Of course, the Lincolns also knew the greatest black leader of the day, Frederick Douglass, who twice met with the President in the White House and attended his second inaugural reception in 1865. After the war, when rumors circulated that Lincoln's widow was in financial distress, Douglass offered to lecture on her behalf. Yet there is no photograph of Frederick Douglass in the Lincoln family album, though he hung a picture of Lincoln in his study. All of the people pictured in the Lincoln album were white—except for a groom holding a horse—and save for celebrities, all were members of the family.

Mary lost her enthusiasm for all but family pictures after the death of Willie Lincoln in February 1862. At first she was prostrate with grief, and soon she began a rigorous mourning that lasted twice as long as even the darkly grim standards of her era required. For over two years she gave up writing to old and fond acquaintances who brought to mind the happier days when Willie was alive.

As late as November 20, 1864, Mary was still reflecting guiltily about Willie's death. "I had become," she wrote to an old friend, "so wrapped up in the world, so devoted to our own political advancement that I thought of little else besides. Our Heavenly Father sees fit, oftentimes to visit us, at such times for our worldliness, how small & insignificant all worldly honors are, when we are *thus* so severely tried." The date of this confession seems startlingly significant: only two weeks earlier, Abraham Lincoln had gained reelection as President of the United States. Such worldly honors as election victories now made Mary nervous rather than happy.[35]

Mrs. Lincoln has been accused of being much concerned for her husband's reelection, not only out of natural pride and persistent ambition, but also from fear that with a sudden change in their income and credit status, he might learn of the enormous personal debts she kept secret from him. This may not be fair or accurate. "My position," she explained in the same letter that described Willie's death as a punishment for her political ambition, "requires my presence, where my heart is *so far* from being." Although Mary outwardly continued her interest in things of the world—secret and conniving correspondence about political appointments, delicious gossip, and expensive fashions—she may well have turned her back on them emotionally. Certainly she collected few photographs of the glittering world around her thereafter. "Our home is very beautiful," Mary explained while in mourning for Willie, "the grounds around us are enchanting, the world still smiles & pays homage, yet the charm is dispelled—everything appears a mockery, the idolised one, is not with us."[36]

Later, when she was a widow, her photograph album suffered downright neglect. One could not ascertain, from looking at the pictures that survive, that Mrs. Lincoln had ever been out of the United States, much less that she lived for extended periods of time in Europe after the Civil War, traveling throughout Great Britain and the Continent. She retained photographs of the executive mansion itself and the Anderson cottage at the Soldiers' Home, the Lincolns' summer residence in Washington. But she seems to have made no attempt to obtain images of the picturesque and historic sites of Europe or of the people she associated with there. Sometimes she attempted to travel incognito, and secrecy would have impeded any friendly exchange of photographs. But for the most part her self-imposed banishment to a "land of strangers," despite her occasional letters describing her travels, amounted to a genuine exile.

As Mary remarked of the White House: "Bidding Adieu, to *that house,* would *never* have troubled me, if in my departure, I had carried with me, the loved ones, who entered the house, with me." Instead, as Mary remembered bitterly, "all the sorrows of my life, occurred there."[37]

What was worse, Mary would soon suffer more tragedies so isolating that she would have no one left to whom to show her pictures. In the grip of desolation, and later, scandal, the surviving Lincolns all but withdrew from the public eye.

Reluctantly, from a quiet sense of stern duty, Robert T. Lincoln later took a modest part in public life and service, but he was the last of the Lincolns to do so. The rest became absorbed in family life and, in some cases, in themselves.

The evidence in the photo album of this perhaps unhealthy turn inward testifies to the self-absorption of the subjects. Gone from later years were the pictures of sites visited on trips and portraits of colleagues and friends. Though Abraham Lincoln never left the United States, except for a few hours he likely spent on the Canadian side of Niagara Falls, most of his family and descendants traveled widely. His widow and his sons Tad and Robert all lived abroad for long periods. Robert's children did too. Yet the family's photographic horizons did not expand accordingly. Instead, they shrank, and one sees only the stingiest glimpses of other persons and places. Robert's wife, on the other hand, kept an album of her own that included cartes of European scenes and celebrities, some of which may have been sent to her by her mother-in-law.

Mary's legacy of family devotion and her touching, uncomplicated love of children became in her later life and in later Lincoln generations a smothering blanket of attachment that stunted the social maturity of some and drove off the lovers of others. Abraham Lincoln's legacy grew ever dimmer. One of the first traits to disappear from the family, naturally enough, was the Lincolnian sense of humor. Instantaneous photography would invite informality, but the later Lincolns seldom displayed before the cameras the nonchalance or charm one wishes their presidential forebear could have had the opportunity to reveal. A later snapshot of his grandson strumming a tennis racquet as he might a guitar stands out among the other staid, occasionally even tortured-looking later portraits. Lincolnian eloquence and literary style—acquired characteristics, surely—also died with Abraham Lincoln. Most important, the simple democratic spirit withered after his departure, and Mary's aristocratic pretensions not surprisingly gained more influence over the family's future.

Mary Lincoln's protracted emotional convalescence after the assassination was certainly sincere and more than understandable in the tragic circumstances. Yet her mourning was so self-conscious and persistent that no fair-minded person can read the letters she wrote after 1865 with unalloyed sympathy. Her sad plight naturally elicited compassion, but Mrs. Lincoln practically *demanded* it. For example, her long-standing dislike of Lyman Trumbull's wife, Julia, led Mary to this acid interpretation of Mrs. Trumbull's visit, at a time when the shattered widow was seeing few callers.

> *I have heard of Mrs. Trumbull, calling, on some in the house, she met, my little Taddie, & did not enquire about me. As a matter, of course, I should not have seen her, without I was seeing every one; cold, unsympathizing persons, are unpleasant enough, when we are happy, but when we are otherwise, their presence is terrible. As they dined, with us last winter, in W—— one, would suppose, the world had taught her, the civilities of life, to speak kindly, to the boy & ask, after the health of his Mother. Even Little Taddie, remarked, the breach of politeness.*[38]

Grief was almost universal among women of Mrs. Lincoln's era. The emotional trials of high infant mortality were com-

pounded in the 1860s by the burdens of widowhood for hundreds of thousands of soldiers' wives. Some have described the especially hard-hit South of the postwar period as a "widows' society." Mrs. Lincoln's afflictions were less unusual than they might seem at first glance: indeed, the law looked upon her husband as a casualty of the war and tried his alleged assassins by a military commission for, among other things, the crime of killing the commander-in-chief of the army and navy of the United States.

Yet the law did not view Mrs. Lincoln as a military widow. She received shabbier treatment than did the ordinary wife of a deceased common soldier; for a time Abraham Lincoln's widow did not even receive a pension. Insecure about money at all times despite her substantial personal wealth (from her husband's estate, comprised mostly of untouched presidential salary of $25,000 a year), Mary grew almost frantic in pursuit of a congressional stipend. Her husband was the first victim of presidential assassination in American history, and his widow therefore became a victim of that circumstance. No one had thought to provide a law for such an eventuality.

Among the rest of the family, Tad became the principal casualty of Mary's bereavement. He had unavoidably suffered neglect from his busy father in the White House. One observer noticed that Tad had been deprived of "care and attention . . . by the duties of office." Now Mary could not bear to have him separated from her, but the indulgences of his youth had taken their toll. He needed schooling and discipline, yet, Mary admitted, "I am so miserable, it is painful to part with him, even for a day." While she lived in Chicago in 1865, Mrs. Lincoln confessed, "Taddie is going to school & for once in his life, he is really interested in his studies—After all, few children learn well, without some one, sharing their lessons—If his darling, precious brother Willie had lived, *he* Tad, would have been much further advanced."[39]

Indeed, Tad was far behind other boys his age. Mary wrote a revealing letter on June 15, 1865 (when Tad was twelve), to the boy's former White House tutor. The tutor knew the truth, and Mary did not need to be vague about the boy's problems. "He says [recites] two or three lessons a day," she assured the teacher, "& is at length seized with the desire to be able to *read & write*—which with his *natural* brightness, will be *half* the battle with him. I hope he will be able to write by fall."

In August 1865 Mrs. Lincoln had to admit to the former tutor that Tad "does not apply himself to his studies, with as much interest as he should." By December 1866 Tad could read—"quite well," as Mary said, "—as he did not know his letters when he came, here [to Chicago], you will agree he learns rapidly." Tad learned, but never far from his mother's orbit. When he died at age eighteen in 1871, he had hardly lived at all.[40]

The differing educational patterns of the children reveal the profound effects of the family's crucible. Robert, the first child, started early, attending schools and academies from about age seven on. Willie was writing poetry at eleven. Tad, by contrast, did not get his real start until 1865, at age twelve, White House tutoring obviously not making much impact, since his indulgent parents were on hand to keep the tutor from taxing the boy. Except for Robert and Robert's son, no one in the family showed any marked diligence or ambition after the death of Abraham Lincoln. And even before Lincoln's death the family's increasing affluence and prominence, as well as the natural reaction to domestic tragedy (the deaths of a short-lived second son, Eddie, in 1850 and of Willie in 1862), dampened the ardor for worldly success and self-sacrifice. Constant pressure from public scrutiny and personal tragedy made the Lincolns turn inward, choosing not to surrender any more of themselves out of fear that the "public" would take and take till there was nothing left.

Robert had already left home by the time of his father's death, though by chance he was in Washington the night of the assassination. Its meaning to him will forever remain hidden behind Robert's emotionless façade. His numbingly unrevealing correspondence tells us little of his inner life, but he was buffeted by fates as terrible and powerful as the ones that his mother experienced. After his younger brother Tad's death in 1871, for example, Robert's "own strength was . . . used up" and he felt "compelled" to leave his law office "for as long a period as possible." Apparently his doctor ordered the time off, and he departed for at least three weeks.[41]

The immediate impact of the assassination on him, six years earlier, is more difficult to assess. Apparently, he found some relief in assuming the role of "noble" son, an adjective his mother more than once applied to descriptions of him in those years. But what he learned about his mother in that period forever altered their relationship. When the executor of the President's estate revealed to him that it was encumbered by Mary's debts, the revelation at first seemed "mysterious" to Robert, who was unaware of any such claims. He soon began to suspect that his mother was insane on the subject of money. In 1867, when Mary disgraced the family by trying to sell her old clothes in New York, Robert warned his fiancée, Mary Harlan, that his mother was "on one subject not mentally responsible." Mary Todd Lincoln attended their wedding in 1868 and then fled for Europe, herself humiliated by the "Old Clothes Scandal" in which the press and public castigated her mercilessly for trying to raise money by selling her used gowns and accessories. Robert grew increasingly distressed by her peculiarities.[42]

Idiosyncrasies notwithstanding, Mary Lincoln welcomed her new daughter-in-law warmly, despite her dislike of Mary Harlan's father. James Harlan, an Iowa senator and ardent Methodist, had gained appointment as Secretary of the Interior from Lincoln near the end of the President's life; in fact, Harlan did not actually assume office until after Lincoln's murder. When, as a widow, Mary Lincoln attempted to persuade the Andrew Johnson Administration to make Anson Henry, an old friend and Lincoln's onetime doctor, the commissioner of Indian Affairs, the Secretary of the Interior refused to comply, and Mary grew furious. "Mr. Harlan, has acted in the most contemptible way! It has become so much so with every one, that when I write to Wash—— on any subject of business, I receive no reply, it is so, with Robert also." When Harlan, who would become Robert's father-in-law, wrote Lincoln's son to explain why Henry did not get the appointment, Mrs. Lincoln sniffed: "Sec Harlan wrote R. a letter, full of all manner of excuses . . . *he* is intensely selfish & I trust, I shall never see any of them again—I am sure, as *we* are not now in power, *they* do not desire it."[43]

Mary did see Harlan again, as father of her son's bride, some three years later. Apparently she visited none of the senator's perceived sins on his daughter. Indeed, just before the wedding Mary regarded "the proposed marriage" as "the only sunbeam" in her "sad future." She had "known & loved the young lady since her childhood, our families have been very intimate and . . . she recently & sweetly expressed herself to me—that she felt, she was only passing from one mother to another." Mother-in-law smothered Mary Harlan Lincoln with gifts and advice.

After the birth of her first granddaughter, also named Mary, in 1869, Mary Lincoln redoubled her attentions, despite a continuing coolness between the in-laws. Though Mrs. Lincoln spoke of "very intimate" relationships between the families and corresponded with the bride's mother, Mrs. Harlan signed her letters "A.E.H." and Mary had no idea what the *A* stood for; she did not even know Mrs. Harlan's first name. Occasionally Mary was too insistent in regard to what the baby should wear or how the younger Lincolns' house should be decorated, but the affectionate grasp did not grow unendurably tight until Mary moved in with her son and his family after the death of Tad in 1871.

Robert later admitted to his aunt that he "had to break up housekeeping to end the trouble" that ensued. "Breaking up housekeeping" was Victorian code for what we would call today a "separation"; in short, Mrs. Lincoln came close to destroying Robert's marriage. Mary Lincoln and her daughter-in-law did not speak again until near the end of Mary Lincoln's life more than a decade later, when she was pathetically broken in health. In this agonizing period of bad relations, the younger Lincolns arranged for Mary to visit her grandchild regularly only when Mary Harlan was not present, but the grandmother used these occasions to denounce the mother to the daughter. Eventually, the aging widow apparently even threatened to kidnap the child to get her away from Mary Harlan Lincoln's imagined bad influence. Not long thereafter, in the spring of 1875, when the elder Mrs. Lincoln began to suffer from hallucinations and exhibit other bizarre behavior, Robert caused his mother to be tried by a Cook County jury to determine her mental state, and she was judged insane and committed to a mental institution.[44]

After she had spent four months in a private sanitarium, Mary and her friends engineered her release. Concentrating on getting out of the institution forced her to focus clearly on what she wanted in life. After she regained nominal control of her finances from Robert's court-ordered conservatorship, she fled back to Europe, partly out of fear that her son might try to commit her again. Robert decided never to do so again, despite his mother's idle threats, voiced in the presence of witnesses, to murder him. Their break was now complete. In a bitter letter written in the summer of 1876, Mary demanded the return of the many gifts she had sent her son and daughter-in-law over the years—paintings, engravings, silver, lace, jewels, books, and silks—now charging they had been stolen. "Two prominent clergy men . . . think it advisable to offer up prayers for you in Church," railed Mary, "on account of your wickedness against me and High Heaven."[45] For a long time, Robert did not even know his mother's address, and he had but one picture of her, the carte de visite illustrated in this book.

If Mary could happily bid adieu to the White House, with its dreadful memories, Robert had even less reason to think of it fondly. He lived a life without illusions. In a moment of revealing candor, he told a man in 1887 who had suggested that Robert run for the presidency that he had "a repugnance to what is called 'public life' that is almost morbid." In his thinking, there were "few men in respectable positions in life less to be envied than a President. There is not the faintest glamour about the place to me." Lincoln knew that his "availability" (which in the nineteenth century meant what is connoted by "electability," "popular appeal," or "name recognition" today) came "in only a very slight degree from anything attributable to myself." He made "not the slightest pretensions" to personal merits as a public man. It was the Lincoln name they were after, and Robert realistically knew it.[46] In the same year he granted an interview to the *Illinois State Journal,* in which he declined consideration for the vice-presidential nomination. As for persistent questions about running for President, Robert commented sharply: "It seems difficult for the average American to understand that it is possible for anyone not to desire the presidency, but I most certainly do not. I have seen too much of it. I can well remember the tremendous burden my father was called upon to bear. I have seen enough of the inside of Washington official life to have lost all interest for it. The presidential office is but a gilded prison."[47]

Mary and Robert had escaped, and there was no looking back. Though an ever-widening emotional gulf separated them from 1865 on and especially after 1875, Robert and his mother were more alike than either recognized at the time. Neither mother nor son cared much for photographs of themselves, and neither liked to see their photographs published for the public. More important, both despised future Lincoln biographer William H. Herndon. Commenting on the inconsequential government post Lincoln had made available to his onetime law partner during the war, Robert said, "My father did offer him a membership on a temporary board of *three persons*—wage five dollars per day—to pass on war supply claims. I suppose the idea was that he could not do much harm, having two decent men to do the work." If Mary regarded Herndon as "a dirty dog" and "almost a hopeless inebriate," Robert for his part thought of him as a "blackguard" of "drunken habits." Both mother and son believed he stole the books owned by Abraham Lincoln that Herndon found mixed in with others in the firm's law library.[48]

Even more striking was Mary's influence on her son's outlook on society. Though some today defend Robert from charges of snobbishness, they are not very convincing. His attitude toward his father's nickname "Honest Abe" provides a case in point. When Robert heard that a book would be published with that title, he attempted to influence the publisher, like Robert a Harvard graduate, to persuade the author to change it. Robert pointed out that "after his youth at least, my father was never addressed familiarly and personally by anything but his last name, even by his most intimate friends." "Honest Abe" was a "temporary and not very widely extended vulgarity" got up by newspapermen in 1860, Robert said. "The fact is that the epithet was the outcome of a state of civilization which did not know how to express itself with propriety." When he was reminded that his father may have been given the nickname in his youth as a storekeeper in New Salem, Robert admitted his error to the publisher but said he "did not think that a serious book about Lincoln ought to have as a title a soubriquet given him when twenty-two years old by the small gang in which he moved at the time, who must have felt themselves a hard lot by indicating that he was the only honest man among them." This Harvard man wanted to put his father's frontier past behind him.[49]

Robert survived the emotionally trying mid-1870s. The trial and commitment of his mother, though widely reported in the press, apparently proved to be no political hindrance, and he accepted appointment as the Secretary of War in James A. Garfield's Cabinet six years later. After the President's assassination, Chester A. Arthur retained Robert in the post. The Republicans lost the next election, but when Benjamin Harrison recaptured the presidency for them in 1888, Robert was made minister to Great Britain the succeeding spring. In 1890, while the family resided in Europe, Robert's only son, Abraham Lincoln II, called Jack, died, apparently from blood poisoning

H. ROCHER   CHICAGO.

contracted from surgery to remove a carbuncle. He was only sixteen years old.

In the wake of Jack Lincoln's death, the Lincoln family's strange pattern was repeated, allowing grief for lost children to be compensated for by an almost suffocating affection for those that remained. In 1892 Robert's first daughter, Mary, nicknamed Mamie, married Charles Isham, an attorney and antiquarian of a retiring nature who was related to Robert's law partner. The second daughter, Jessie, eloped in 1897 with an Iowa Wesleyan football player and sometime minor league baseball player named Warren Beckwith, of whom Robert decidedly did not approve. When the marriage ended in divorce ten years later, Beckwith blamed it on his mother-in-law, who, he maintained, was so lonely after Jack Lincoln's death and the departure of her daughters from home that she interfered with his marriage, attempting often to get his wife, Jessie, and their children, a new generation named Robert and Mary, away from him. When Mary Harlan Lincoln took Jessie and their children to London with her, about a year after the birth of Robert "Bob" Beckwith, Warren sued for divorce on grounds of desertion and won. There was likely more to the story than what one of the interested parties in the divorce said, but Beckwith's complaint seems plausible. He gained a divorce easily enough in an era when it was difficult. Ironically, grandmother Mary Harlan Lincoln thus followed in Mary Todd Lincoln's footsteps, for years earlier Mary Todd had wanted to remove Mary Harlan's daughter from one of her parents, too.

Beckwith's story is one of the few fragments of evidence available about the extremely private descendants of Abraham Lincoln. Although Jessie married twice again, once to a geographer named Johnson and finally to an electrical engineer named Randolph, she does not appear to have left the sphere of her family, especially her mother, Mary Harlan Lincoln.

Except for the obvious hold she kept on her daughters, not much is known about Mary Harlan Lincoln. She was so reclusive that Robert seemed always to be making excuses for her and declining invitations. Her withdrawal was so complete, in fact, that a recent biographer of Mary Todd Lincoln has accused her daughter-in-law of alcoholism.[50] One is tempted to paraphrase the old joke about General Grant's drinking and prescribe a barrel of whatever Mary Harlan drank—because she lived to be ninety years old!

A more plausible explanation of Mary Harlan Lincoln's close confinement to home, besides the customary reticence of Abraham Lincoln's heirs, was neurasthenia, a vague psychosomatic illness suffered by many upper-class women of her generation. One refuge from this paralyzing malady might have been religion, and Mary Harlan Lincoln embraced a religion almost tailored for neurasthenic women and other chronic sufferers: Christian Science. Perhaps by denying the existence of her illness as she grew in spiritual strength, Mary Harlan Lincoln overcame her suffering. No one will ever know, but Christian Science did leave a lasting impression, for one third of the sizable estate left by her children went to the Christian Science Church.

The family album bears witness to Mary Harlan Lincoln's reclusiveness: there are only three pictures of her in it, and only two of them are formal portraits. Likewise, her apparent inability to get along with her sons-in-law is apparent in the complete absence of pictures of any of them: Charles Isham, Warren Beckwith, Frank Johnson, or Robert J. Randolph.

And of the next and final generation, almost nothing can be said. So little is known of Lincoln Isham, Bob Beckwith, and Peggy Beckwith that to write about them is surely to distort their lives. They did not want to be written about, and they did not offer the public any documentary record on which to base an essay. Almost anything that appeared in the press about them was an accident or aberration, and reconstructing their lives from the few clippings available is surely perilous.

The last generation of Lincolns was nearly a century removed from their famous ancestor, but in terms of upbring-

ing, wealth, regional affiliation, and professional ambition could as easily have been separated by a millennium.

The eldest but least known of the group, Lincoln Isham, was the only child of Mary "Mamie" Isham and her millionaire husband, Charles. Born in New York City in 1892, he dropped out of Harvard, a newspaper reported, because "his frail body was unequal to the strain." Later, he is said to have performed secret work for the government during World War II. He married a New York "society girl" named Leahalma Correa, and helped raise her daughter, Frances Mantley. The Ishams had no children of their own. Little else is known about Lincoln Isham, except that he died on September 1, 1971, in Dorset, Vermont, where he had lived on a twenty-two-acre farm. Isham left the bulk of his estate to the Red Cross, Salvation Army, and American Cancer Society, plus a $440,000 trust fund to his stepdaughter. He sent his great-grandmother Mary Todd Lincoln's "chicken leg coffee set" and a few other pieces of White House china to the Smithsonian, and the rest of his family artifacts were sold at auction.[51]

Warren and Jessie named their first child Mary Lincoln Beckwith, but she was called Peggy. As with Abraham Lincoln II, the family seemed to have trouble even speaking their famous names, much less pursuing the same ethic of public service. Peggy was born August 22, 1898, in the Harlan hometown, Mount Pleasant, Iowa. In 1930 a journalist described her glowingly as "a scholar, farmer, and scientist," explaining that she had just taken a "short but intensive course at Cornell" and had begun applying it to raising cattle at Hildene, the Vermont estate her grandfather, Robert, had built and which she now occupied. For a time, Peggy seemed headed toward a career as an aviatrix. "The spirit of Abraham Lincoln lives," the same journalist gushed, "and in his great-granddaughter, Miss Mary Lincoln Beckwith, many of his outstanding characteristics continue." But although she built a private landing strip near Hildene and purchased several planes, little is known of Mary's life as a pilot after the early 1930s; evidently it was not noteworthy.[52]

Unlike her great-grandmother, Peggy did "not care for elaborate clothes," and most photographs show a dowdy, overweight woman who bears some physical resemblance to Mary Todd Lincoln. And like the first Mary, she was not adverse to offering occasional controversial opinions. Unfortunately, most were ill advised, and a few downright presumptuous. In 1954, for example, she declared that if Lincoln were alive "he would be an Eisenhower Republican." A few years later she betrayed a woeful ignorance of Lincoln lore when she used the occasion of a U.S. navy decision to build sister nuclear submarines called *Abraham Lincoln* and *Robert E. Lee* to say of her ancestor, "I think he would have liked that. You know, they were good friends, though they didn't agree politically."[53] She was entirely wrong.

Peggy ventured into dangerous territory during the civil rights ferment of the early 1960s, when she told journalists that she disapproved of Attorney General Robert Kennedy's "aggressive" desegregation policies. "Bobby Kennedy is just too impetuous on this whole integration question," she asserted in 1963—ironically, the centennial year of her great-grandfather's Emancipation Proclamation, not to mention his "all men are created equal" declaration at Gettysburg. "This is a good time to reflect, and I think Abe Lincoln would do a lot of reflecting himself if he were here," Peggy hinted. "We're Southerners," she explained. "The aggression of the federal government in forcing integration concerns me." But asked point-blank whether she was suggesting that Lincoln would have shared her "concern," she wisely admitted, "I can't say. I'm as far away from him as anyone else."[54] Even more wisely, Peggy publicly ventured no further opinions on such matters for the rest of her life.

Her political sympathies appear to have been representative of the clan. Grandmother Mary Harlan Lincoln was apparently a Republican, as the New York *Times* reported her application for membership in the Wendell Willkie Club in 1940.[55] Peggy certainly seems to have been a Republican, and so was her brother, Bob.

Lovingly
Bob

Mary Lincoln Beckwith died quietly in 1975, leaving the Hildene estate and $425,000 in Lincoln family cash to the Christian Science Church, in the hope that Robert Lincoln's home could become "an historical museum open to the public."[56] Only after sufficient funds were raised privately was the house rescued from its legatee so that Peggy's dream could be fulfilled.

Perhaps the most perplexing of the fourth generation of Lincolns was Peggy's younger brother, Robert Todd Lincoln Beckwith, who admitted years later to an interviewer, "I'm a spoiled brat."[57]

Born on July 19, 1904, near Chicago, Bob was an indifferent student, passing through two unremarkable years at his grandfather Robert's alma mater, Phillips Exeter, before drifting in and out of a prep school in Washington, D.C., and a military academy somewhere in New York. He did not attend college but is said to have received a degree from the National University Law School, although he would later list his profession not as attorney but as "gentleman farmer of independent means." During World War II he served in the coast guard, a stint that gave him a lasting interest in boating.

Bob managed to avoid publicity most of his life; when he failed, the results occasionally proved embarrassing. Newspapers of 1925, for example, were filled with smiling pictures of the young man after his arrest for speeding in Omaha.[58] He said little to the press, save that his hobby was boats. Later he added fast cars and women to his list of interests.

Judging from his love life, he did not exaggerate. His first marriage, which lasted thirty years, was to an older widow whose son was only ten years younger than his new stepfather. Washington newspapers reported that "it was a common sight . . . to see 'Bob' or 'Buddy' Beckwith drive up in his flivver, accompanied by his young stepson, James Raymond Wilson. The two are friends and constant companions."[59]

After the first Mrs. Beckwith's death, Robert married again at age sixty-three, this time to a twenty-year-old West German named Annemarie Hoffman. The marriage ended not only in divorce but in a flurry of supermarket tabloid headlines. Newspapers had a field day reporting the effort by Mrs. Beckwith to have her son, Timothy Lincoln Beckwith, declared her husband's legal heir. Robert countered with proof that he had undergone prostate surgery and a therapeutic vasectomy, and sued for divorce on the grounds of adultery. The would-be heir to the Lincoln name and fortune failed to prove Robert's paternity, and his mother took him back to Germany.[60] Robert Beckwith later married a third and final time to Margaret Fristoe.

Beckwith attended occasional Lincoln functions. He met President Eisenhower at the White House, visited Gettysburg and Springfield, sat in the room at the Library of Congress as the Abraham Lincoln papers were unsealed, and was honored at Lincoln College in rural Illinois for his "personal uniqueness and rich family heritage." He told the press he had visited the New York World's Fair and found the Walt Disney talking Lincoln figure "wonderful."[61]

Robert donated much of what remained of the family archives to the State of Illinois—including the valuable letter books containing copies of some twenty thousand letters from his grandfather Robert T. Lincoln's personal correspondence. He also allowed historians access to the so-called insanity file his grandfather had preserved to help prove his wisdom in seeking his mother's commitment. And it was Robert Beckwith who preserved the Lincoln family album.

Beckwith spent his last years, sadly, wasting away from Parkinson's disease at a Saluda, Virginia, nursing home—only forty-five minutes away from the old Confederate capital of Richmond. The last of Abraham Lincoln's descendants died there on December 24, 1985, at the age of eighty-one.

When reporters promptly asked his attorney whether her client had ever shared any insights into his family legacy, she responded: "We didn't talk about anything like that. Socially, it's not done."[62] If Beckwith knew any family secrets, he took them to the grave.

And the same was true of the other Lincoln descendants. About all that can be safely said of them is that, after Mary Todd Lincoln, not a single one of them ever attempted to exploit their famous ancestor's name. On the contrary, after Robert T. Lincoln, they seemed to shun their past and live for the present. Robert's hobby, after all, was astronomy—a scientific interest not unlike his father's forward-looking interest in technology. In religion and lifestyle, they joined the modern age willingly, as Jessie's and Bob's three marriages apiece surely suggest. She ran off with a sports hero, her son fancied fast cars and boats, and her daughter grew interested in aviation. Except for Mary Harlan Lincoln's interest in Christian Science, religion ceased to be much of a factor with the family after Mary Todd Lincoln's death. Robert Lincoln's religious views certainly seem vague; and Peggy Beckwith had no service at her death—her ashes were spread over her estate. These people were not interested in the past, not even in their own family's past, and it seems to have annoyed them a little to find that so many strangers were.

Bob Beckwith lived in a world of blissful self-imposed ignorance about his great-grandfather. In the only extended interview he gave, "the small man with the balding gray hair and the warm, shy smile" confessed that he had never been very interested in the subject of Abraham Lincoln, and never would be. The most memorable Lincoln-related event of his life he could recall at the time had occurred years before when a tourist at the Lincoln Memorial stumbled against his parked car. The car, he explained to the perplexed interviewer, had been a Lincoln, too.

When the reporter tried to probe more deeply, not bothering to disguise her incredulity that the little old man claimed not an iota of special connection to his illustrious ancestor, Robert Todd Lincoln Beckwith—the great-grandson of Abraham Lincoln and his last direct descendant—simply sighed: "I just want to live my own life."[63]

He did.

THE
FAMILY
ALBUM

This is the Lincoln family album, Abraham and Mary Lincoln's own leather-bound photograph book, which the President and his wife kept with them in the White House to collect portraits of family, friends, and celebrities. Like others of this highly popular style, it was designed to display the latest portrait craze sweeping Civil War America: the small, visiting-card-size pictures introduced first in France, and so known here by their French name, cartes de visite. By 1864, the third year of the war, a New York journal would report:

> Everybody keeps a photographic album, and it is a source of pride and emulation among some people to see how many cartes de visite they can accumulate from their friends and acquaintances.... But the private supply of cartes de visite is nothing to the deluge of portraits of public characters which are thrown upon the market, piled up by the bushel in the print stores, offered by the gross at the book stands, and thrust upon our attention everywhere. These collections contain all sorts of people, eminent generals, ballet dancers, pugilists, Members of Congress, Doctors of Divinity, politicians, pretty actresses, circus riders, and negro minstrels.

The Lincoln family drew the line at minstrels, pugilists, and ballerinas, but otherwise collected an eclectic variety of photographs. On the pages that follow—in addition to the unique family ambrotypes taken before the carte was introduced, and the cabinet photos and Kodak snapshots that became popular later in the century—are some of the pictures this album once held: of politicians, members of Congress, eminent military heroes, even a Barnum star. Side by side with these celebrities are the pictures of family and friends, the same species of portrait that graced similar albums in less exalted households in the 1860s.

ABRAHAM LINCOLN, AGE FORTY-EIGHT— WITH HIS "WILD REPUBLICAN HAIR"

This is Abraham Lincoln in 1857, two weeks after his forty-eighth birthday—still a year away from capturing the national spotlight at the Lincoln-Douglas debates. It is the family's only copy of the famous picture, a mirror-image 2¾ × 3¼ inch, or sixth-plate tintype of the original taken on February 28, 1857, by Chicago photographer Alexander Hesler. The portrait is enclosed in a decorative brass mat and framed in a book-style morocco case. It was produced not by Hesler but by William Haven Masters of Princeton, Illinois, who probably photographed it later on tin from a surviving Hesler paper print; Hesler's original negative had perished in the Chicago fire.

This almost rustic portrait presented not only the "awkward bonhommie of his face," in the words of one contemporary, but also "its thatch of wild republican hair . . . the irregular flocks of thick hair carelessly brushed" across the "shaggy brow." Lincoln himself admired the likeness, pronouncing it "a very true one," but his wife, Mary, a stickler for dignity, did not. Lincoln explained that her "objection arises from the disordered condition of the hair."

The tintype was presented to Robert T. Lincoln in 1885 by a local widow in whose home his father had stayed in 1856. The old lady was convinced, along with many of her Princeton neighbors, that Lincoln had sat for Masters in Princeton that day, with this image the result.

LINCOLN'S FIRSTBORN SON, ROBERT— "LIKE HIS MOTHER, A TODD"

While I was a boy at Springfield . . . [a] new process came in, called the ambrotype," Robert T. Lincoln recalled sixty years after this picture was taken. "I have an ambrotype of myself made in 1858. It is made of glass, having a backing of wax of some sort. One operation produced only one portrait." This is the portrait. At the time it was taken, as one Springfield friend of the family remembered, Robert was, "like his mother, a Todd, in appearance and disposition."

He was fifteen years old and enrolled in the Illinois State University, which despite its name was a small preparatory school where, Robert admitted later, "we did just what pleased us, study consuming only a very small portion of our time."

ROBERT THE EXETER STUDENT— "A NEAT-LOOKING BOY" WITH "A HOMELY FATHER"

When this ninth-plate ambrotype was taken, in 1859 or 1860, Robert T. Lincoln had failed his admission tests for Harvard. Resolving "not to retire beaten," he agreed to enroll at Phillips Exeter Academy in New Hampshire, where a classmate remembered "Bob" as "a neat-looking boy, a favorite in the school and popular with the girls."

Robert's father came to New England on a speaking tour in February 1860. Robert was in the audience with his friends when Abraham Lincoln walked onto the stage of Exeter's town hall, his hair standing "in all directions." One girl in the crowd was heard to whisper, "Isn't it too bad Bob's got such a homely father." But ten minutes into his speech, the audience fell under Lincoln's spell. "We forgot all about his looks."

It was around this time, Robert later wistfully recalled of his father, "when I would have had both the inclination and the means of gratifying my desire to become better acquainted with the history of his struggles." But Robert would go on to Harvard, his father to the White House. "Henceforth," he said, "any great intimacy between us became impossible."

As for his mother, Mary Lincoln claimed she missed Robert terribly when he left home, but thinking back on their first separation many years later, after their break, she insisted acidly, "it was a great relief to us all, when he was sent East to school, *then* we had a most loving peace."

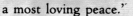

BABY OF THE FAMILY

The Lincolns' fourth and youngest son was born in 1853 and named for his father's father: Thomas Lincoln. But practically from birth, his parents called the new baby Tad, because his large head made him resemble a tadpole.

Not long before this sixth-plate ambrotype was taken, probably in 1858, Mary referred to herself cheerfully as "the mother of three noisy boys," of whom Tad, undisciplined and, for a time, ineducable, was doubtless the noisiest. To Mary he was nevertheless "our *dear little Taddie.*"

One photographer of the day particularly dreaded sessions with such restless little boys: "What cake crumbs, nut-shells and candy paper from the hands of their fathers, were by these little ones lavished at will upon my carpet."

WILLIE AND TAD—
LINCOLN "LOVED
WHAT THEY LOVED AND
HATED WHAT THEY HATED"

These companion quarter-plate ambrotypes, framed in a hinged thermoplastic case, were taken in Springfield around 1859, when Willie (left) was nine, and Tad, six. Believing that "a rare-ripe child quickly matures, but rots as quickly," Lincoln doted on his boys and refused to discipline them when they ran wild, which was often. On Sundays, his law partner William H. Herndon bitterly recalled, Lincoln turned his "little devils" loose in their office. "They soon gutted the room, gutted the shelves of books, rifled the drawers, and riddled boxes, battered the points of my gold pens against the stairs, turned over the inkstands on the papers, scattered letters over the office, and danced over them." Herndon was convinced that "had they s——t in Lincoln's hat and rubbed it on his boots, he would have laughed and thought it smart." His partner was "blinded to his children's faults," Herndon complained, adding: "He worshipped his children and *what* they worshipped; he loved what they loved and hated what they hated."

LINCOLN AT THE FRONT

On October 2, 1862, Abraham Lincoln paid a surprise visit to the headquarters of the Army of the Potomac near the site of its recent victory at Antietam. The President hoped to prod his cautious commander, George B. McClellan, into mounting a new campaign against the Confederates.

Photographer Alexander Gardner, then in Mathew Brady's employ, caught up with the presidential party on October 3 and made a series of staged pictorial records of Lincoln's visit. In this pose, Lincoln towers above both Allan Pinkerton (left), McClellan's intelligence chief, and General John A. McClernand, one of McClellan's subordinates. Longtime Lincoln intimate Ward Hill Lamon, who accompanied the party to Antietam, remembered that when Lincoln stood at his full height "he stooped slightly forward," maintaining an expression, vividly apparent in this pose, that reflected "silent reveries . . . not sorrows of to-day or yesterday, but long-treasured and deep,—bearing with him a continual sense of weariness and pain."

This uncropped print (note the towels hanging on the tree at left, and beneath them, the photographer's assistant holding a slate with the plate number) may well be Lincoln's own copy. For years it hung in a simple old frame on the wall of Robert Lincoln's study at his Vermont country estate, Hildene.

THE CHANGING FACE OF TAD LINCOLN

Tad Lincoln was the "chartered libertine" of the White House, according to presidential secretary John Hay. But the shock of his father's assassination left him "greatly sobered," as the photo, top, taken around 1868, suggests. Three years later, just before his death at age eighteen in 1871, Tad had changed even more dramatically, as the photo, bottom, reveals. "Years . . . spent in study and travel," observed Hay, had "produced an utterly different person." In his place had emerged this "well-grown young gentleman." By the time these photographs were taken, Tad no longer resembled a Todd, either. With an elongated face and suddenly prominent nose, Tad looked more like his father.

A ABRAHAM LINCOLN II ON HIS DEATHBED

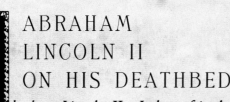

Abraham Lincoln II—Jack to friends and family—lies on his deathbed in this Kodak snapshot. It was taken in 1890 in London, where Jack's father, Robert Lincoln, served as minister to the Court of St. James. Jack's health was in alarming decline, despite two operations. The surgery, for what newspapers of the day called a "malignant carbuncle" under the armpit, was not considered dangerous, but Jack developed blood poisoning, rallied bravely but briefly, then slipped into a coma and died on March 5, 1890, at age sixteen. Queen Victoria sent a message of sympathy to Robert, while, back in America, Jack's surviving grandfather, former Senator James Harlan, mourned: "And so my coal is quenched—both Mr. Lincoln's and mine." He was referring to the late President: Jack was Abraham Lincoln's only male descendant in his generation.

When these last pictures of Jack were taken, possibly by his sister, Mamie, revolutionary Kodak cameras had taken the country by storm, launching a new age of amateur photography. Each roll of paper film took up to one hundred pictures, but to get them developed, the owner had to send the entire camera to Rochester, New York, where the film was unloaded and processed, the 2½-inch circular prints were mounted on cards, the camera reloaded, and the entire package mailed back—all for ten dollars.

W. Scott

J. Holt

R Anderson

R Anderson

BREVETÉ S.G.D.G. F.R.G. PATENT

LEAF FROM THE FAMILY ALBUM

This is a page from the original Lincoln family album, as the 130-year-old relic looks today—now stripped of the original photographs it once displayed, but still bearing the penciled-in names of the people whose portraits once inhabited it. This close-up view of an original leaf from the empty album shows in detail its ornate, violet-colored decorative scrollwork, a feature that suggests that the Lincolns' album was of particularly good quality. The album itself is owned by the Illinois State Historical Library in Springfield. The photographs from the album are in the collection of the Louis A. Warren Lincoln Library and Museum in Fort Wayne.

"THE OLD FAMILIAR FACE OF A. LINCOLN"

Samuel M. Fassett took this picture in Chicago on October 4, 1859, when Lincoln, seven months away from the presidential nomination, was fresh from a triumphant speaking tour of Ohio. Observing him there, the Cincinnati *Enquirer* described "a dark-visaged, angular, awkward, positive-looking sort of individual with character written in his face . . . a Western man."

The day after Fassett took this picture, Lincoln moved on to Clinton, Illinois, where a local journalist reported: "The old familiar face of A. Lincoln is again amongst us, and we cannot help noting the peculiarly friendly expression with which he greets everybody, and everybody greets him. He comes back to us after electrifying Ohio, with all his blushing honors thick upon him; yet the poorest and plainest amongst our people, fears not to approach, and never fails to receive a hearty welcome from him."

Describing the Lincoln he knew at the time, law partner William H. Herndon recalled a face "long, narrow, sallow, and cadaverous, flesh shrunk, shriveled, wrinkled, and dry," with "a few hairs here and there; his cheeks . . . leathery and saffron-colored."

"WHAT A PLEASANT HOME ABE LINCOLN HAS"

This "modest-looking, two-story brown frame house," in the words of a reporter who visited during the 1860 campaign, was the only home Abraham and Mary Lincoln ever owned. The Lincolns purchased it in 1844, two years after their wedding, from the minister who had married them. The cost was $1,500 in cash and land. To *Frank Leslie's Illustrated Newspaper* it seemed during

the presidential race "the simple home of . . . [an] American statesman," while a Utica, New York, paper exclaimed, "What a pleasant home Abe Lincoln has." During that campaign summer—throughout which the candidate followed tradition and stayed close to Springfield, saying nothing new—Lincoln posed outside the house for this John Adams Whipple photograph, which subsequently served as the model for widely reproduced parlor prints and newspaper woodcuts—for a century a popular scene that put great emphasis on hearth and home.

The photo was also issued in both large and carte-de-visite photographic editions, and was republished—like this copy—after Lincoln's assassination, when demand for images associated with him was renewed. Lincoln can be seen standing rigidly inside the front yard, gripping one of the fence rails to steady himself for the lengthy exposure. Willie stands next to his father, but moves his head; his portrait is blurred. Impish Tad peers out from behind one of the corner posts. The neighbors congregating on the primitive wooden sidewalk have never been identified.

S. P. TRESIZE, - - Enterprise Gallery,
SPRINGFIELD, - ILL.

MRS. LINCOLN'S ELDEST SISTER

After the death of their mother in 1825, Mary's eldest sister, Elizabeth, became the most important person in her life: teacher, friend, and surrogate mother. In 1832 Elizabeth married Ninian Wirt Edwards, then a college student in Lexington, Kentucky, and moved to Springfield. Mary, unhappy living with her stepmother, followed Elizabeth to Springfield in 1839, taking up residence at the Edwards home.

When Lincoln courted Mary in their parlor, Elizabeth recalled that he "would listen and gaze on her as if drawn by some superior power." Nonetheless, Elizabeth and Ninian advised the couple not to marry. As Elizabeth later explained: "They were raised differently and had no congeniality, no feelings, etc., alike." Eventually, Mary and Lincoln were wed anyway, in the Edwards home, on November 4, 1842. Mary could detect "little *weaknesses*" in her sister but in 1861 had to admit that Elizabeth was "the only one of my sisters who has appeared to be pleased with our advancement."

MARY'S SISTER AND BROTHER-IN-LAW, THE LINCOLN FAMILY DOCTOR

The Lincolns were undoubtedly close to Frances "Fanny" Todd Wallace, Mary's sister, and they named their third son, William Wallace Lincoln, for her husband, William (below). He was one of Springfield's physicians. Dr. Wallace's partner later remembered that "Mr. Lincoln was always very solicitous when his boys were sick . . . his sympathy was almost motherly," and their doctor became important to Lincoln, who felt that he owed Wallace much.

This family album photograph of the Lincolns' family doctor was taken in Washington, after the President had made William Wallace a paymaster in the Union army. Mrs. Wallace later wrote a generous reminiscence of the Lincoln marriage, contending that "they did not lead an unhappy life at all . . . he was certainly all to her a husband could have been."

MARY'S HALF SISTER AND HER HUSBAND

Margaret Todd Kellogg (left) was Mary Lincoln's half sister—one of nine children by their father's second marriage. For a time they seemed particularly close, even after Margaret married and moved to Cincinnati. She attended the Lincolns' last reception in Springfield, subsequently turned up at the White House when the Lincolns moved in, and stayed more than three weeks, along with other Todd relatives.

Like other Todds, Margaret expected an Administration patronage plum for her husband, preferably a foreign assignment, where Charles could be closer to his brother, the painter Miner Kilbourne Kellogg, then working in Europe. That autumn, Mary expressed indignation that "Kellogg . . . did not know why he had *not* received his appointment as *Consul*," adding snidely: "Is not the idea preposterous?" Lincoln consoled him with an army job.

LINCOLN'S "PARTICULAR FRIEND"

Burly, two-fisted giant Ward Hill Lamon—"Hill" to friends—was one of the few Illinois cronies Lincoln took with him to Washington. Back in the 1850s the Virginia-born lawyer had ridden the circuit with Lincoln. A tireless political worker for Lincoln in 1860, not only did he join the family for its long inaugural journey, but he alone accompanied the President-elect on a secret midnight passage through hostile Baltimore. Lamon armed himself for the task with two revolvers, a knife, and brass knuckles.

Although Lincoln made Lamon marshal of the District of Columbia, his greatest contribution came in his efforts to guarantee Lincoln's safety. Fearing particular danger in 1864, Lamon began sleeping outside Lincoln's bedroom door. Ironically, Lincoln had dispatched him on a mission to occupied Richmond only days before his assassination. The night Lincoln was shot, the man he called "my particular friend" was in the capital of the defeated Confederacy.

Lamon's friendship with the late President's family ended abruptly in 1872 when he published a ghostwritten, surprisingly critical Lincoln biography. The book angered Robert and wounded Mary by describing the Lincoln marriage as so unhappy that "neighbors and friends, and ultimately the whole country, came to know the state of things in that house." Lashing out at Lamon's "vile, unprincipled and debased character," Mary said of the "infamous" book: "I have not seen it, nor should allow it, to be brought into my presence." Surprisingly, this carte of Lamon, almost certainly added to the family collection while Lincoln lived, was never expunged from the album after the family rebuked him.

POLICITAL INTIMATE

O f all Lincoln's political allies, none was more loyal than Jesse K. Dubois (left)—"one of his closest and most intimate friends," Dubois's son recalled. Dubois met Lincoln when both served in the Illinois state legislature in the 1830s. Lincoln thought he had "the elegant manners of a Frenchman, from which nation he had his descent." In 1860 Dubois helped manage Lincoln's nomination for President. It was Dubois who wired Lincoln from the Chicago convention (the candidate had stayed home in Springfield): "Moving heaven & earth nothing will beat us but old fogy politicians." After the election, Dubois expected to become a patronage dispenser in his home state, but Lincoln repeatedly disappointed him. Nonetheless, Dubois never wavered from the pledge he had given his friend in 1854: *"I am for you against the world."* He named one of his sons Lincoln; another became a U.S. senator.

A NEW LOOK FOR THE NEW PRESIDENT

A beard of several months' growth covers (perhaps adorns) the lower part of his face," the New York *World* alerted the nation in early 1861, around the time this photograph was taken by C. S. German in Springfield. Shown here is the family's later copy (in a size larger than the carte de visite of the Civil War era) made by local Springfield photographer F. McNulty. During the campaign, an eleven-year-old admirer named Grace Bedell had—among others—written to the candidate imploring him to improve his appearance by covering more of his face with whiskers. In a famous reply (page 61), Lincoln protested that people would regard it as "a piece of silly affect[at]ion" were he to start a beard so late in life. But soon after his victory, start one he did.

Lincoln told a sculptor for whom he was then sitting that he posed for this photograph "to present [it] to a very dear friend." As a journalist covering the President-elect perceptively noted of the supposedly camera-shy Lincoln: "He knows that those who elected him are anxious to see how he looks, and hence is willing to gratify . . . their excusable curiosity."

Springfield, Ills Oct 19. 1860

Miss Grace Bedell

My dear little Miss.

Your very agreeable letter of the 15th is received—

I regret the necessity of saying I have no daughters— I have three sons— one seventeen, one nine, and one seven, years of age— They, with their Mother, constitute my whole family.—

As to the whiskers, having never worn any, do you not think people would call it a piece of silly affectation if I were to begin it now?

Your very sincere well-wisher

A. Lincoln

In her letter to presidential candidate "A B Lincoln," little Grace Bedell informed him, "I have got 4 brother's and part of them will vote for you any way and if you will let your whiskers grow I will try and get the rest of them to vote for you you would look a great deal better for your face is so thin." Besides, Grace added, "all the ladies like whiskers and they would tease their husband's to vote for you and then you would be President." This is Lincoln's famous reply. Only a few weeks after writing it, he began to sport whiskers after all. Four months later, traveling through southwestern New York State on his long journey to Washington for his inauguration, President-elect Lincoln stopped briefly in Grace's hometown and asked to meet her. Then, as a crowd of onlookers erupted into "yells of delight," Lincoln bent from his great height and gave her "several hearty kisses."

Springfield, Ills. Oct 19. 1860

Miss. Grace Bedell
My dear little Miss

Your very agreeable letter of the 15th. is received.

I regret the necessity of saying I have no daughters. I have three sons—one seventeen, one nine, and one seven, years of age. They, with their mother, constitute my whole family.

As to the whiskers, having never worn any, do you not think people would call it a piece of silly affect[at]ion if I were to begin it now?

Your very sincere well-wisher.

A. Lincoln.

THE PRINCE OF RAILS

Here was the perfect nickname for the son of the country's new ruler. His British counterpart, the Prince of *Wales,* was on a widely heralded American tour. Meanwhile, stories of Abraham Lincoln's early life as a railsplitter were capturing the popular imagination. It was not surprising that a letter would soon be delivered to Harvard student Robert in Springfield, addressed only: "His Royal Highness, the Prince of *Rails.*" The sobriquet caught on quickly.

Home from college to accompany his family to Washington, "the heir apparent," as a newspaper wag dubbed him, was "observed of all the observing Springfield girls," with "the effect of a residence within the improving influences of genteel, well dressed and well behaved Boston . . . plainly noticeable in his outward appearance." His Aunt Elizabeth Edwards also noticed the change, writing that Robert "has grown very much and is particularly agreeable." Conceded his father, "He promises very well, considering we never controlled him much." Nonetheless, the New York *Herald* soon reported that "Bob, the Prince of Rails," was "sick of Washington and glad to get back to his college." In photo opposie, he poses in a handsome outfit, and what appear to be leather gloves.

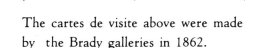

The cartes de visite above were made by the Brady galleries in 1862.

"THIS DAMNED OLD HOUSE"

Every President since John Adams had lived in the White House, and when the Lincolns arrived to take up residence in 1861, one staff aide quipped that it had "the air of an old and unsuccessful hotel." Mary's cousin thought its "deplorably shabby furnishings" looked as though they "had survived many Presidents." Deciding it was "a degradation" to live in such surroundings, Mary launched herself on a monumental redecorating spree, purchasing china, books, carpets, drapes, wallpaper, and new furniture, and modernizing plumbing, heating, and lighting. Ultimately, she exceeded a $20,000 congressional appropriation by $6,700, and when Lincoln found out, he *"swore"* angrily to the Commissioner of Public Buildings that "he would never approve the bills for *flub dubs for that damned* old house! It was he said furnished well enough when they came— better than any house *they* had ever lived in—& rather than put his name to such a bill he would pay it out of his own pocket!" The platform surrounding the flagpole was probably erected for a troop review or parade.

Nicolay

WHITE HOUSE SECRETARIES

By today's standards, Lincoln's White House staff was minuscule. Most of the work—running the office, handling correspondence, and scheduling appointments—was performed by these two men, twenty-nine-year-old personal secretary John George Nicolay (top) and his twenty-three-year-old assistant, John Milton Hay (bottom). Lincoln called his serious, introspective senior aide "Nicolay," but fondly referred to Hay as "John."

The Bavarian-born Nicolay had been an Illinois newspaper publisher before Lincoln recruited him during the 1860 campaign. After his victory, when correspondence swelled to fifty letters daily, Nicolay enlisted Hay, a friend of Robert's; both young men accompanied Lincoln to Washington.

This Nicolay carte de visite from the family album is the work of an unknown photographer. The rakish portrait of Hay is by the Bierstadt Brothers of New Bedford, Massachusetts. Hay apparently enjoyed exchanging "cartes" with White House visitors, or so he wrote in his diary, a famous "inside" source for the history of the Lincoln Administration, which irreverently refers to Lincoln as "the Tycoon" and Mrs. Lincoln as "the Hell-Cat."

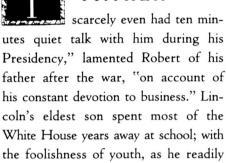

"A STRIKING CONTRAST TO . . . HIS PRESIDENTIAL FATHER"

"I scarcely even had ten minutes quiet talk with him during his Presidency," lamented Robert of his father after the war, "on account of his constant devotion to business." Lincoln's eldest son spent most of the White House years away at school; with the foolishness of youth, as he readily admitted later, Robert threw away the letters his father sent to him there.

Personality differences may also have contributed to the growing gulf between them. A reporter who observed father and son in 1861, the year this carte de visite was taken, noted in Robert's "comparative elegance" a "striking contrast to the loose, careless, awkward rigging of his Presidential father." Unlike his father, Robert presented a refined public image, one effusive New York journalist calling him "a young man of . . . much dignity . . . a dutiful and affectionate son." Posed like a European dandy, Robert even appears to be clutching a handkerchief.

The date inscribed on the back of his photograph—July 24, 1861—offered the first clue to the precise day of a sitting that included Robert's brothers. All the pictures at the session can be identified by the distinctive striped rug on which Robert stands for this pose. But the photographer remains unknown.

I "MORE VALUE TO THEIR FATHER... THAN ANYBODY KNEW"

n a White House perpetually gripped by civil and military crisis, there was "but one brightness" that gave it "almost a home-like look," recalled staff aide William O. Stoddard: Lincoln's younger boys, "who came and went . . . at their own childish will." There was Willie (top), a "peculiarly promising boy," and little Tad, "full of merry mischief, the ludicrous effect of which was in no way lessened by the impediment in his speech whenever he was called to account"—which was "not very often." Stoddard recalled the day Tad discovered "the place where all the bell-wires in the house were attached to a central pinion," setting off "all bells, and human answerers of bells, in futile motion." Even the more serious Willie, he added, was not above slitting "into ribbons the cloth covering of the private secretary's table."

Another observer recalled them as opposites: Willie, "intelligent, polite, observant," and Tad, "overflowing with the joys of his young life and almost constantly near and clinging to his father who never appeared to be annoyed by his freaks and capers."

Stoddard saw "both or either come and stand by their father's knee, at times, when grave statesmen and pompous generals were presenting to him matters of national or world-wide importance." Such diversions, Stoddard believed, "were of more value to their father and to his work than anybody knew."

A TAD WITH THE HERO OF FORT SUMTER

lthough this photograph of Tad has been published many times before, no one seems to have noticed on the table next to him the carte de visite of the hero of the day, Major Robert Anderson, the defender of Fort Sumter. Anderson is also shown here in a photo published by C. D. Fredericks in New York in 1861.

As the defender of the Union fort in Charleston harbor whose fall on April 15, 1861, started the Civil War, Anderson emerged as one of the first military celebrities of the Civil War. Lincoln invited him to the White House two weeks later (and eventually his picture was added to their family album). There Tad, who was rarely discouraged from bursting in on official visitors, may have met Anderson. The Lincoln boys became infatuated with military heroes, and their parents had little uniforms made for them.

Ample evidence exists that Tad liked photographs both of himself and of his heroes. Playing in the White House one day with his little cousin Katherine Helm, Tad "showed her a photograph of himself with great pride," according to an eyewitness, and then, "picking up one of his father, said, 'This is the President,'" punctuating his announcement with a shout of, "Hurrah for Abe Lincoln!"

Entered, according to Act of Congress, in the year 1861, by C. D. Fredricks & Co., in the Clerk's Office of the United States for the Southern District of New York.

Presidential secretary John Hay called Tad Lincoln "the tricksy little sprite who gave to that sad and solemn White House . . . the only comic relief it knew." Evidence of that impish spirit can be glimpsed in this July 1861 carte, for which Tad posed in a miniature Zouave uniform, perhaps modeled after those worn by the troops of Elmer E. Ellsworth, the recently martyred family friend (see page 71).

Tad irreverently disfigured his own image with an inked-on mustache and goatee, as he would a photograph of himself taken years later after the war, as a teenager. Such jokes were typical of the boy, who was so bursting with "pranks and fantastic enterprises," in Hay's words, as to seem an "infant goblin." Even his doting mother referred to Tad as "my little troublesome *sunshine*." The family retained an unaltered copy of this photograph as well.

UNION MARTYRS

These men symbolized the struggles to end slavery and preserve the Union: Senator Charles Sumner (left), the Massachusetts abolitionist viciously caned by a Southern congressman on the Senate floor in 1856; and Colonel Elmer Ephraim Ellsworth (right), the dashing young Zouave who became the first commissioned officer killed in the Civil War. Each was close to the Lincoln family.

During the war, Sumner became chairman of the Foreign Relations Committee, and a critic of Lincoln's sluggishness on emancipation. He also became a friend of Mary Lincoln, who revered the elegant, intellectual New Englander. Mary described White House visits when "that cold & haughty looking man to the world—would insist upon my telling him all the news & we would have such frequent and delightful conversations & often late in the evening—my darling husband would join us & they would laugh together like *two* school boys." To his credit, Sumner did not drop Mary after Lincoln's death. He not only continued to correspond with her, he lobbied for five years to secure her a congressional pension.

Ellsworth had been a law student in Lincoln's Springfield office in 1860. He also commanded a brilliantly costumed Zouave cadet group. Ellsworth grew close to Lincoln—"as intimate," the President acknowledged, "as the disparity of our ages, and my engross-

Brady,   Washington.

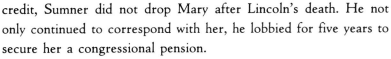

ing engagements, would permit." Ellsworth traveled with the family to Washington for the inauguration, then accepted a federal post that would keep him close to them. But when war broke out, Ellsworth organized an 1,100-man Zouave unit comprised of New York firemen and returned looking resplendent in "red cap, red shirt, grey breeches, grey jacket," and "in his belt, a sword, a very heavy revolver, and . . . bowie knife . . . with body enough to go through a man's head from crown to chin as you would split an apple."

On May 23, 1861, Colonel Ellsworth was killed in Alexandria. Immediately lionized as the Union's first Civil War martyr, Ellsworth was given a White House funeral. The President wrote a touching letter of condolence to Ellsworth's parents—a "tribute to the memory of my young friend, and your brave and early fallen child. . . . In size, in years, and in youthful appearance, a boy only," wrote Lincoln, "his power to command men, was surpassingly great." To the President, Ellsworth was "the best natural talent, in that department, I ever knew."

This Ellsworth carte, its background added by an artist, is the work of Silsbee, Case & Co. of Boston; the Sumner portrait is by the Brady Gallery in Washington. There were several cartes of each man in the family album.

 "COUSIN LIZZIE"

Elizabeth Todd Grimsley (right) was one of Mary's favorite relatives, a friend since childhood and later a bridesmaid at the Lincoln wedding in 1842. "Cousin Lizzie," as both Lincoln and Mary affectionately called her, married a Springfield man in 1846.

Fifteen years later she traveled to Washington for the inauguration, enjoying round after round of White House social events. She remained for a full six months, as Lizzie explained it, because "Mary hates to be alone" and "urged and urged" her to postpone her departure. Like other Todd relatives, Lizzie was also seeking Administration patronage: a postmistress job for herself, which was not offered, and a Naval Academy appointment for her son, which was.

Mary remained close to the cousin she variously described as "very sweet" and "noble." For the President's wife, Lizzie exemplified "the memory of those who were so kind to me in my desolate childhood."

ANOTHER TODD, ANOTHER DEMOCRAT

Lizzie Grimsley's brother, Captain Lockwood M. Todd, was another of the Todd relatives who surged into Washington in March 1861 for their in-law's presidential inauguration. Lockwood stayed six weeks, enough time to pose at Mathew Brady's gallery for this remarkably candid photograph with the Lincoln children, Willie and Tad. Like most of the other Todds, Lockwood was a Democrat and had not supported Abraham Lincoln for the presidency, but he expected an appointment from Lincoln anyway.

VIEW FROM THE WHITE HOUSE

Sculptor Clark Mills, who would make a somber-looking life mask of President Lincoln in 1865, was probably best known for this heroic statue of Andrew Jackson. It stood inside Lafayette Park, directly across the street from the White House lawn; the Lincolns could see it from the upstairs windows.

The statue was considered an engineering marvel in its day but as a work of art it was controversial. When the English novelist Thackeray first saw it, and was told by an enthusiast that Mills had accomplished it without ever having observed another equestrian sculpture, Thackeray commented, "To see other statues might do Mr. Mills no harm."

This carte de visite by John Goldin is one of several scenes of Washington that Mary collected. In addition to her photographs of the White House and the Capitol, which are illustrated in this book, the collection included views of the War Department, the Treasury Building, the Post Office Department, and the Smithsonian.

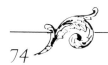

G "DOWN TO MT VERNON"

eorge Washington's Mount Vernon sat just across the Potomac River, not far from the Union capital. But it became part of the Confederacy on April 17, 1861, the day Virginia voted to secede. Only weeks before, Mary Lincoln had taken a small group "down to Mt Vernon," as she reported to a friend, referring to it as "a visit we can again pay, when you are with us." Because of the war, however, she did not return for another year—this time on an excursion with the entire family and what the newspapers referred to as "a party of personal friends." Mary may have purchased this carte de visite—along with additional views of the house and another of Washington's tomb—on one of those visits.

The century-old Mount Vernon was in terrible condition at the time. "The ravages of time and the rust of neglect," according to one visitor, were "rapidly destroying" the landmark. In 1864 one of Mount Vernon's regents protested against Union interference with the steamboat run from Washington, which was the Mount Vernon Ladies' Association's sole source of income after the war interrupted its fund-raising. Lincoln urged Secretary of War Stanton to allow the outings to resume, but Stanton thought it imprudent at the moment. Mary's photograph of the house is marked on the back in her hand: "Mansion at Mt Vernon/East front."

T A TODD—BUT NO RELATION

his man may have seemed as important as any Todd in the Lincolns' lives during the early days of the Civil War—even though he was no kin to Mary. Captain Henry B. Todd led the "Lincoln Cavalry," a unit that guarded the capital in the summer of 1861. In a reconnaissance in Virginia that autumn, he allowed his men to straggle and loot in hostile territory. The unit suffered several casualties, and Todd himself was captured. After he was exchanged for a Confederate prisoner of war, Todd returned to duty in Washington, but this time his superiors put him in a desk job: provost marshal of Washington. He spent most of his time administering prisoners in the notorious Old Capitol prison.

Capt, Henry B Todd
Co. B. Lincoln Cavalry

"IDOLIZED CHILD OF THE HOUSEHOLD"

"Willie was the favorite," recalled one of the boys' Springfield friends, "being, like his father, very companionable and democratic in his manner." He struck his Aunt Emilie as "a beautiful boy; intelligent, polite, observant, careful of the comfort of others and courtly in his manners." Even Mary characterized Willie as "the idolized child, of the household." And cynical White House secretary John Hay would concede that "with all his boyish frolic" Willie was "a child of great promise, capable of close application and study," something never said of his younger brother.

Mary admitted that his death left her irretrievably "visited by affliction." Years later she could think of him only as "my Angel boy, in Heaven." Recalling his photographs, Mary told an artist: "You have doubtless heard, how *very* handsome a boy, he was considered—with a pure, gentle nature ... *far, far* beyond his years."

MARY TODD LINCOLN— IN "THE FIERY FURNACE OF AFFLICTION"

This is the only photograph of Mary Lincoln in the entire family album. Taken in the fall of 1863, it shows the forty-five-year-old mistress of the White House elegantly jeweled, but still dressed in deep mourning for Willie. His death had sent Mary into what she described in a poignant mixed metaphor as "the fiery furnace of affliction" and "the *deep waters*" that threatened to "overwhelm" her. This grim portrait shows that time had not eased her pain.

At her gayest, Mary would impress a journalist with her "fair, cheerful, smiling face, which does one good to look upon." But contemplating one of her graver photographs, women's rights advocate Lydia Maria Child thought she looked "mean and vulgar" and "more like a dowdy washerwoman . . . than like the 'representative of fashion.'"

Mary spent lavishly on her clothes and accessories, yet seldom sat for photographs. "My hands are always *made* in *them*, very large," she complained, "and I look too stern." As her sister put it, she "was opposed to having her face scattered abroad." Indeed, when the E. & H. T. Anthony Co. of New York prepared to reproduce some of her old Brady cartes de visite, Mary wrote quickly to say "You will certainly oblige me" by having them "destroyed."

On the back of the sole image the family retained in its album, Robert wrote: "Return to the Hon. R. T. Lincoln," suggesting that he would surrender this picture only temporarily to comply with requests from publishers for suitable family illustrations.

THE SUMMER WHITE HOUSE

Mary called this house "a very charming place 2½ miles from the city, several hundred feet, above, our present situation." For three summers the Lincoln family made its home here, a fifty-year-old, multi-gabled, twelve-room "cottage" on the grounds of the Soldiers' Home north of Washington. Dubbing it the "Presidential country-house," one visitor described it as "situated on a beautifully wooded hill . . . shaded on both sides by widespread branches forming a green arcade above you." The shade and high ground made it a welcome refuge from Washington's torrid heat.

With two companies of troops guarding them there, Mary wrote a friend, we "can be as secluded, as we please." This became especially important after Willie's death. "When we are in sorrow," she explained, "quiet is very necessary to us."

For a while Lincoln commuted to and from the city alone on horseback; later, he was guarded by soldiers. Observing him "coming in to business" on one such August morning, Walt Whitman, then an army nurse, described him as "dress'd in plain black, somewhat rusty and dusty," looking "about as ordinary in attire . . . as the commonest man," except for the "company of . . . cavalry, with sabres drawn, and held upright over their shoulders."

Mary was no doubt looking forward to returning to the summer White House in 1865, but her husband was assassinated that April. Writing to a friend four months later from stifling Chicago, she reminisced: "How dearly I loved the 'Soldier's Home['] & I little supposed, one year since, that I should be so *far removed* from it, broken hearted, and praying for death."

All she had left was this souvenir carte de visite by Washington photographer John Goldin. Mary labeled it on the back: "President's House at 'Soldiers Home.'"

A CONFERENCE OF WAR WITH McCLELLAN AT ANTIETAM

A companion pose to the photograph of Lincoln with Pinkerton and McClernand (see color section), this superb large portrait of the commander in-chief in a conference of war with his top general was also taken by Alexander Gardner at the headquarters of the Army of the Potomac in Maryland Heights on October 3, 1862. It is likely Lincoln's own copy of the photograph.

The pale President and the battlefield-ruddy commander pose at a table cluttered with battle maps and reports, while on the ground beneath it lies a captured Confederate banner. One cannot avoid the impression, perhaps overlooked in the 1860s, that most of the props—the American flag tablecloth, for one—had been carefully arranged by the photographer. The photographer was not privy to what were surely tense conversations between the two men. Less than a month after the meeting, Lincoln dismissed the commander some called "the Little Corporal of Unsought Fields," a decision that no doubt pleased Mary, who thought the general "a humbug . . . because he talks so much and does so little."

Enter'd according to act of Congress, in the year 1862, by ALEX. GARDNER, in the Clerk's Office of the District Court of the District of Columbia.

SECRETARIES OF WAR

These two men each served as Secretary of War in the Lincoln Administration, and both their portraits were kept in the family album. When Simon Cameron of Pennsylvania (top) resigned after a year amid criticism for incompetence and rumors of department-wide corruption, Edwin M. Stanton (bottom) quickly became one of Lincoln's closest advisers.

Mary was far friendlier with Cameron, turning to him several times for special favors and military commissions for her acquaintances. After the assassination of Lincoln, Cameron tried to launch a relief fund for the widow's benefit and later argued emotionally on the Senate floor for her pension. Mary referred to Cameron as "a kind tender hearted man," and "a *true friend* . . . not unforgetful, as so many others, have been, of the kindness, of my beloved husband."

Mary enjoyed far less success ingratiating herself with Cameron's unsentimental and incorruptible successor. Even the President admitted that Stanton "does not always use the most conciliatory language." Lincoln thought Stanton "a brave and able man," but Mary found him "irritable."

After Stanton's death, when Republican money men took up a collection to aid his impoverished family, Mary responded with a jealous tirade—tempered, however, with respect even she could not deny her husband's tireless minister. "I . . . dearly loved Mr. Stanton," she wrote, "& greatly appreciated the services he rendered . . . our loved, bleeding land, during the trying rebellion. Yet he died peaceably on his bed. . . . My husband, great, good & glorious, *beyond* ALL WORDS of praise—was cruelly murdered." The family album also boasted cartes of most of the other men who served in Lincoln's Cabinet over the years.

REBEL IN THE WHITE HOUSE

Emilie Todd Helm was Mary Lincoln's half sister, the fifteenth of their father's sixteen children. Emilie, whom Lincoln called "Little Sister," was eighteen years younger than Mary and only seven years older than the Lincolns' son Robert.

Although Mary left their father's house when Emilie was three, she got to know the young woman later when she arrived for a visit at the Lincolns' Springfield home. There Emilie found that Mary "mothered her husband as she did her children, and he seemed very dependent on her."

In 1856 Emilie married West Point graduate Ben Hardin Helm. When war broke out in 1861, Lincoln offered him a Union command, but Helm joined the Confederate army instead and was killed at Chickamauga in 1863. Although Lincoln confided that he "did not wish it known," he invited the young widow and her daughter, Katherine, to the White House, where he and Mary greeted them with "the warmest affection."

But the visit soon became awkward. Emilie and Mary were unable to "open our hearts to each other as freely as we would like," Emilie confessed in her diary. When the wounded Union war hero General Dan Sickles heard she was resident in the Executive Mansion he went directly to Lincoln to complain, "You should not have that rebel in your house." Emilie left soon thereafter, armed with a presidential pass designed "to protect her against the mere fact of her being Gen. Helm's widow." Lincoln had to revoke it the following summer, saying he never intended "to protect her against the consequences of disloyal words or acts." Mrs. Helm responded with a bitter letter, reminding Lincoln "that your . . . *bullets*" had transformed her into "a woman almost crazed with misfortune." Emilie outlived even Robert, who kept this photograph of his aunt framed on the wall of his Vermont home.

AMERICA'S BEST-KNOWN CLERGYMAN

Henry Ward Beecher was probably the most famous churchman in the North. The son of minister Lyman Beecher and brother of Harriet Beecher Stowe, author of *Uncle Tom's Cabin,* Beecher used his pulpit at the Plymouth Congregational Church in Brooklyn to speak out forcefully against slavery.

It was Beecher who invited Lincoln to speak in New York in 1860, offering a $200 honorarium, which Lincoln accepted. "I took it, *and did not know it was wrong,*" Lincoln later explained, after the stipend became a campaign issue. But the resulting address at the Cooper Union in Manhattan helped propel him toward the presidency.

Lincoln also attended services at Beecher's church in Brooklyn. Observing him in a pew there, "his body swayed forward, his lips parted . . . entirely unconscious of his surroundings," an onlooker heard Lincoln "frequently giving vent to his satisfaction" with Beecher's sermon "with a kind of involuntary Indian exclamation,— 'ugh!' "

Impressed with the clergyman, Lincoln insisted "there was not upon record, in ancient or modern biography, so *productive* a mind, as . . . Henry Ward Beecher."

Beecher could count Mary Lincoln as an admirer, too. On her first trip outside Washington in May 1861, Mary, with Cousin Lizzie in tow, made a point of attending services in his church. Then or soon afterward, Mary no doubt acquired the two cartes of Beecher that she inserted into her White House album.

AMBASSADORS, ARISTOCRATS, AND A FUTURE KING

L ong considered a diplomatic Siberia, Washington nonetheless teemed with astute ambassadors and colorful aristocrats during the Civil War. Mary Lincoln, who could speak some French, enjoyed hobnobbing with Washington's foreign colony.

Among the foreign dignitaries who added glitter to life in the capital or at least portraits to the pages of the family album were Richard, Lord Lyons (top left), who became British minister to the United States in 1858 and remained at his post throughout the war; and Albert Edward, Prince of Wales (top right), eldest son of Queen Victoria, and the future King Edward VII, who became in 1860 the first member of Britain's royal family to visit America.

Joseph Charles Paul Bonaparte (bottom left) Napoleon Bonaparte's nephew, was known to Washington as Prince Napoleon. Mary Lincoln threw a White House reception in his honor following his dramatic arrival in Washington aboard his own yacht. That evening the White House committed the ultimate faux pas, as the band struck up the *Marseillaise* even though its incendiary lyrics had been banned by the Second Empire. The prince proved his diplomatic finesse by laughing: *"Je suis Républicain—en Amérique!"*

Baron Edward de Stoeckel (bottom right), Russia's ambassador to Washington, represented a country that at the time was one of the Union's most dependable allies.

UNUSUAL WHITE HOUSE VISITORS

Lincoln's White House opened its doors to countless visitors during the war, but none more unusual than the world-famous midget Tom Thumb and his wife (right) and the colorful frontier trapper Seth Kinman (opposite).

Mary hosted a reception for fifty special guests in honor of the Barnum attractions, "General" and Mrs. Thumb, on February 13, 1863, and both the three-foot, four-inch Tom and his bride, Lavinia, were invited to stay in the mansion overnight. As P. T. Barnum would appreciatively write some years later, "Abraham Lincoln's cheerfulness," evident on such occasions, proved "invaluable to him in the trying years of our civil war." The Anthony Co. carte of *General Tom Thumb and Wife* bears on the back the facsimile inscription: "Compliments of Charles Stratton/ Lavinia Warren Stratton," the real names of Barnum's stars. They probably handed this copy to the Lincolns during their visit. In a frequently quoted backstairs memoir, Mary's seamstress insisted that Robert haughtily refused to attend the Thumb reception, huffing to his mother, "my notions of duty, perhaps are somewhat different from yours." But when Robert's own Harvard photo album was examined,

General Tom Thumb and Wife.

found therein was his own carte de visite of a midget couple, suggesting a less rigid attitude after all.

In November of 1864 California hunter Kinman arrived to present Lincoln with a unique gift, a hideous chair fashioned by the frontiersman from the horns of elks he had bagged himself. The Kinman photograph by Brady was published in 1864. The family album also contained a separate carte of the elkhorn chair; both photographs were probably given to the President during Kinman's visit.

Civil War artist-correspondent Alfred R. Waud sketched the White House ceremony on the morning of November 26, 1864, at which time hunter Kinman presented his chair to the President. Apparently the chair itself was too complicated even for Waud to draw on the spot. He left out the details, substituting instructions to his publisher, the pictorial newspaper *Harper's Weekly*: "put chair in here." (*Library of Congress*)

SETH KINMAN,
California Hunter and Trapper, who presented President Lincoln with the Elk Horn Chair.
Entered according to Act of Congress by Seth Kinman, in the year 1864, in the Clerk's office of the District Court
Brady   of the District of Columbia.   *Washington.*

AN ACCIDENT— THEN A NEW ENGLAND VACATION

Following a carriage accident in July 1863, and a painful recuperation in oppressively hot Washington, Mary Lincoln traveled to New England to regain her health, taking Tad and Robert with her. A reporter who observed Mary on the trip that followed noted her "very easy, agreeable way," suggesting that she was well along the road to recovery. So did the moment captured in this hitherto unpublished photograph.

When it was taken, as the inscription on the back indicates, Mrs. Lincoln's party was visiting Franconia Notch, one of the most dramatic of the glacial formations that dot the New Hampshire landscape. Here they pose on a perilous-looking, narrow wooden walkway along the tower wall of "the Flume," the best known of the local gorges, and a particularly popular tourist attraction. Mrs. Lincoln is probably standing somewhere in the group, and Tad can be seen squeezing into the crowd at center. Robert stands far off to the left. The overall result is quite candid, or as nearly so as primitive photographic technology permitted at the time.

Lincoln was eager to have his wife come home (see letter). Although she was away from Washington for weeks, Robert later said that his mother "never quite recovered from the effects of her fall."

The President wrote several letters to Mary while she was on vacation, the earlier ones assuring her she should remain away as long as she wished, the later ones urging her with increasing impatience to return to Washington. The very day after writing this inviting note, Lincoln was even more direct: "I really wish to see you." *(Illinois State Historical Library)*

Washington, D.C., Sept. 21, 1863

Mrs. A. Lincoln
Fifth Avenue Hotel
New York

The air is so clear and cool, and apparently healthy, that I would be glad for you to come. Nothing very particular, but I would be glad to see you and Tad.

A. Lincoln

TAD ASTRIDE HIS SOUTH AMERICAN PONY

During the summer of 1864 Lincoln telegraphed his family, vacationing again in New England, "All well, including Tad's pony and the goats." This is probably the pony to which he referred. With Willie dead, Tad became the White House's "absolute tyrant," in John Hay's words, spoiled by a father who gave him "everything he could no longer give Willie," including a menagerie of pets. Tad "thought very little," Hay remembered, "of any tutor who would not assi[s]t him in yoking his kids to a chair or in driving his dogs tandem over the South Lawn."

In a more admiring vein, Hay conceded that Tad "had that power of taming and attaching animals to himself, which seems the especial gift of kindly and unlettered natures."

Henry F. Warren took this photograph of Tad on a Washington street, not long before Lincoln left to deliver

the Gettysburg Address. Some years later, Tad gave it to Robert, inscribing it on the back (see illustration): "Presented to Robert T. Lincoln by his affectionate brother, Thomas Lincoln, a carte-de-visite of himself & new South American pony, as taken Nov 16th, 1863, Washington D.C."

John Hay remembered Tad as a "fearless rider, while yet so small that his legs stuck out horizontally from the saddle," and Walt Whitman recalled often seeing Lincoln riding through Washington in his open barouche, Tad "riding at his right on a pony."

"IMMORTAL-IZED" WITH "THE PREST."

Went ... to Gardner's Gallery," presidential secretary John Hay wrote in his diary on Sunday, November 8, 1863, "& were soon joined by Nico[lay] and the Pres[iden]t. We had a great many pictures taken.... Nico & I immortalized ourselves by having ourselves done in group with the Pres[iden]t." Seen here is the result of that sitting, Hay's personal copy of Alexander Gardner's "group." Lincoln kept a print, too, and Robert inherited it, but after many years of display in bright sunlight, it has faded so badly that it can no longer be effectively reproduced.

Nicolay, who later maintained that "there are many pictures of Lincoln; there is no portrait of him," remembered that the long legs and huge hands visible in this portrait "fitted to this unusual stature, and harmonized perfectly with it." To Nicolay, "the beholder felt that here was a strong man, a person of character and power." Nicolay and Hay went on to collaborate, decades later, on a ten-volume history of the Lincoln Administration, and Hay became U.S. Secretary of State.

March 1864

When this picture was taken in March 1864, the nation was concluding three years of war—and Robert, four years of Harvard. Once he graduated, he began waging a battle of his own: to win permission from his parents to enlist. Lincoln, who was willing to approve, courted political danger that election year by acceding to Mary's wishes that their son be kept out of the military. "I know that Robert's plea to go into the army is manly and noble and I want him to go," she told the President one day within earshot of her cousin, Emilie. "But oh! I am so frightened he may never come back to us." Lincoln pointed out that "many a poor mother, Mary, has had to make this sacrifice." For a while, he gave in anyway. Not until January of 1865 did Lincoln finally convince Mary that Robert could safely join the army.

In a letter to General Grant which Lincoln asked him to read "as though I was not President, but only a friend," he asked whether his twenty-one-year-old son might, "without embarrassment to you, or detriment to the service, go into your Military family with some nominal rank." Grant quickly responded that he would be "most happy" to accommodate Robert, and named him a captain and assistant adjutant general of volunteers.

ARCH RIVAL

Stephen Arnold Douglas, the "Little Giant" of antebellum politics, was Lincoln's arch rival for nearly thirty years. After Lincoln defeated Douglas and two others for the White House in 1860, his lifetime foe proved gracious, calling on the President-elect when he arrived in Washington and praising his conciliatory inaugural address on the Senate floor. That night, when Mary made her triumphant entrance at the inaugural ball, it was on Douglas's arm. When the war began in 1861, Douglas launched a western tour to campaign against secession. After he died in Chicago that June at age forty-eight, Lincoln ordered government offices closed on the day of his funeral and had the White House draped in black. In the years to come, Lincoln maintained occasional contact with Douglas's widow, the former Adele Cutts, and no doubt it was she who gave these cartes de visite to the Lincolns, autographing both and dating them June 1864.

Adele had been the toast of prewar Washington when she became the senator's second wife. One visitor to their home gushed that it was impossible to decide which deserved more praise, "the genius of the husband or the beauty of the wife."

Some biographers have suggested that the first object of Douglas's affections was none other than Mary Todd. And years later, when Mary thought back to "our little cotérie in Springfield during the days of my girlhood," she admitted that such "choice spirits" as Douglas had been "the habitués of our drawing room." But "my great and glorious husband," she hastened to add, was "a world above them all."

Posing with Adele are Robert and Stephen Douglas, the senator's sons by his first marriage.

Stephen A. Douglas
June 1st 1864.

Very truly your friend
&
Adele Douglas
Douglas Place
June 1st 1864.

A ONE OF LINCOLN'S FAVORITE POETS

Abraham Lincoln loved poetry—Shakespeare and Robert Burns especially, but also some modern Americans, including William Cullen Bryant, John Greenleaf Whittier, and this man, the prodigiously talented Oliver Wendell Holmes. Included in his first volume of poetry was a rather maudlin work entitled "The Last Leaf." Several visitors to the Civil War White House would testify to Lincoln's admiration for it. To artist Francis B. Carpenter, for example, Lincoln declared it "inexpressibly touching," particularly this verse:

> The mossy marbles rest
> On the lips that he has pressed
>   In their bloom;
> And the names he loved to hear
> Have been carved for many a year
>   On the tomb. . . .

"For pure pathos, in my judgment," Lincoln said, "there is nothing finer than those six lines in the English language!" Private secretary John Hay added that when Lincoln recited the lines—always with "intense relish"—he gave "the marked Southwestern pronunciation of the words 'hear' and 'year,' " providing a touch of the comic to the sentimentalism.

Holmes wrote an influential article on photography published in the *Atlantic Monthly* in 1862, asserting that "card portraits, as everybody knows, have become the social currency, the 'greenbacks' of civilization." Holmes believed that "the picture tells us no lie" about the sitters. "There is no use in their putting on airs; the make-believe gentleman and lady cannot look like the genuine article."

In this carte de visite from the family album, Holmes looks the genuine article: a cultivated Boston Brahmin exuding wealth, education, and talent.

GENERAL-IN-CHIEF

To the President, Ulysses S. Grant was a commander of "almost inestimable service" to the Union, but Mary Lincoln did not share that opinion. On one occasion the President and his wife were overheard squabbling about Grant's virtues and vices. After listening to his wife enumerate the general's weaknesses, the exasperated President finally retorted: "Well, mother, supposing that we give you command of the army. No doubt you would do much better than any general that has been tried."

During her widowhood, Mary grew even more angry at the war hero she now referred to as "that *small specimen* of humanity." Furious that his admirers were now showering him with gifts while she languished in imagined poverty, Mary angrily charged: "My husband, *did* the great work of the war, *but* Grant, had all the *pecuniary* compensation."

Tad Lincoln, 1864

A page from Carpenter's scrapbook shows the well-known photograph of Lincoln and Tad (center) that the artist adapted for his painting of the family, along with the family album photograph of Willie (lower left) that Mary sent to him to copy. Among the other images pasted onto this page is a photograph of a rival composite family print (lower right), which achieved far more commercial success than the Carpenter project.

A COMPOSITE FAMILY PORTRAIT

Abraham Lincoln posed twice before studio cameras with his youngest child, Tad, but never with his wife or his other sons. After his assassination in 1865, however, Americans clamored for portrayals of the Lincoln family together, eager to visualize the war-weary leader as they imagined he looked in the comforting bliss of domestic life—even if, in reality, such refuge rarely existed for him.

To overcome the absence of a group photograph that could be used as a model, many engravers and lithographers created composites, based on available portraits of individual family members. Most of the results were awkward and inaccurate, but one composite family scene was both carefully researched, artistically assembled, and modeled in part on pictures from the Lincoln family album. Commissioned soon after the assassination, it was the brainchild of artist Francis B. Carpenter, who had painted a group portrait from life of Lincoln's first reading of the Emancipation Proclamation to his Cabinet.

Mary proved eager to help Carpenter, but when the artist asked her to pose for a new photograph, she declined, explaining that "it would be utterly impossible for me, in my present nervous state." Instead she urged Carpenter to consult what she termed "an excellent painted likeness of me ...in a black velvet" by Brady, a flattering, generously retouched early image of a thinner Mary. The "best likeness" of Robert, she advised, was the 1864 work of John Goldin, but "we have none, unframed," valuable proof that the family not only owned but at one time displayed the Goldin pose (Carpenter nonetheless chose a different model). Mary did enclose photographs of Tad and Willie, taking care to point out that "even, in *that* likeness, of Willie, justice, is not done him, he was a very beautiful boy, with a most *spiritual* expression of face."

Mary proposed that Carpenter use this 1861 likeness as his model, and he did, making a mirror-image copy and posing her seated.

Mary thought this handsome likeness by Goldin (top) was the best portrait of Robert. It was later used for the engraving, but for the painting . . .

. . . Carpenter instead used this earlier, clean-shaven Robert as his model (bottom).

Carpenter did not require Mary's assistance to obtain model photographs of the President with Tad, because he had composed the sitting at Brady's Washington Gallery the day the famous photograph of them together had been made.

Carpenter went on to abandon the realistic for the mythical, painting the Lincolns while the family was intact—before Willie's death shattered both parents. The cult of the family, rather than documentary realism, prevailed. Unfortunately, Carpenter took so long to complete his paintings that his patron, New York engraver John Chester Buttre, felt compelled to alter the portrait of Robert for the 1867 print adaptation, for by then, just as Mary's Goldin photograph showed, the one-time Prince of Rails had grown an adult-looking mustache.

Carpenter's painting of the Lincoln family, seen here along with the models from which he worked, stands as the definitive, fully sanctioned portrait—the closest thing we have to a family album portrait of husband, wife, and children together.

Carpenter laid out the design for his painting in this small sketch, which he later pasted in his scrapbook and preserved. Below it he inserted a drawing of a standing Lincoln, which he may have sketched for yet another painting, never accomplished.

Carpenter's chiaroscuro oil portrait emphasized domestic harmony and, with the fruit on the table and the books in Lincoln's lap and at his side, suggested nourishment both physical and intellectual. The Gothic windows in the background are an anomaly in the neoclassical Executive Mansion. (*New-York Historical Society*)

J. C. Buttre's 1867 mezzotint adaptation fashioned Robert's portrait from the Goldin photograph after all, and omitted the sword symbolic of the Civil War from Willie's grasp. Buttre spent $1,164.50 to publish the print, not including Carpenter's $500 fee.

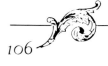

THE "NEW"
U.S. CAPITOL

When Lincoln took the oath of office for the first time on March 4, 1861, the cast-iron dome that had long crowned the U.S. Capitol had recently been dismantled. In its place had risen a lattice of scaffolding and the first evidence of the great tiered dome that was to replace it. War notwithstanding, work proceeded on the dome as well as on the new north and south extensions.

At one point Lincoln ventured a personal opinion about a relief sculpture that was taking shape atop the entrance to the Senate wing. He took an ex-railsplitter's offense at Thomas Crawford's depiction of a woodchopper, complaining that "he did not make a sufficiently clean cut" in the sculpture.

On a "dark and drizzly" March day in 1865, Lincoln stood before the completed Capitol dome to be sworn in for a second term as President. This John Goldin & Co. carte de visite from the family album is marked in ink on the reverse: "Capitol Dome/Wastn," an indication, perhaps, of how important the dome's completion was to the Lincolns. The much mocked, neoclassical statue of Washington by Horatio Greenough, visible from the rear in the foreground, was later moved to the Smithsonian.

TWO
TRAITORS
AND AN
ASSASSIN

With no photographs in their newspapers to satisfy their curiosity, many Civil War–era Americans purchased cartes of the nation's enemies, not just its heroes. Apparently the Lincolns shared this curiosity. Included in the family's trove of old pictures were these three images (from left): Confederate commanding general Robert E. Lee, Confederate President Jefferson Davis, and Lincoln's assassin, John Wilkes Booth.

It is difficult to imagine which Lincoln acquired the undated Booth carte, adapted from an original photograph by Charles D. Fredricks of New York. Robert, who once complained that an insensitive custodian at the family home in Springfield had "orna-mented" its mantel with yet another "picture of Wilkes-Booth," was surely an unlikely purchaser, but the Lincolns did apparently receive many unsolicited pictures sent to them, and perhaps this was one.

On the other hand, the J. Hall & Co. Davis caricature carte, which dates to 1863 and mocks Lincoln's Richmond counterpart over the Confederacy's double defeat at Gettysburg and Vicksburg, could well have been owned by Lincoln himself, who loved a good joke.

As for the Lee pose, a copy of a Minnis & Cowell original taken in Richmond early in the war, Lincoln surely did not purchase it, but he may have held and examined it. On the last day of his life, over family breakfast at the White House on April 14, 1865, Mrs. Lincoln's seamstress recalled that Captain Robert Lincoln, just returned from the front bursting with news of the Appomattox surrender ceremony, showed his father a photograph of Lee. This may be the very pose.

SURRENDER OF
VICKSBURG.
RETREAT FROM
PENNSYLVANIA
FOURTH OF JULY.
1863.

John W. Booth

" HOW HAPPY COULD I BE WITH EITHER ! "
Entered according to act of Congress, in the year 1863, by
. HALL & Co., in the Clerk's Office of the District Court of
he United States for the Southern District of New York.

The Lincoln Family Album

A "DAY OF INDIGNATION" FOR LINCOLN IN ILLINOIS

When news of Lincoln's death reached Illinois on the Saturday before Easter 1865, countless towns promptly shut down businesses and public buildings, organizing public tributes and memorial services. Several were called "Days of Indignation," combination rallies and religious meetings where expressions of outrage joined with prayers for peace.

The meeting in Bloomington, Illinois, was captured in this extraordinary, eight-inch-by-six-inch photograph by J. R. Tankersley on Sunday, April 16, "a Sabbath well spent," declared the headline in the local newspaper. Bloomington's "Day of Indignation" ceremony took place in front of the McLean County Court House, where Lincoln had appeared many times as an attorney before the war. In spite of the rain (note the cluster of umbrellas visible in the picture) some six thousand people squeezed into the courthouse square to respond to the "heart sickening news" of the death of "one of our own." Those who could not get inside perched on the fence in the foreground or stood in the horse-drawn carriages parked outside.

Men wore black and white ribbons of crape, and "the ladies . . . appeared in large numbers in mourning." Prayers were offered from a rostrum beneath which hung a sign declaring, "There is a Balm in Gilead," a poignant answer to the mournful verses from Jeremiah: "How can I bear my sorrow/I am sick at heart . . . /I am wounded at the sight of my people's wound, /I go like a mourner, overcome with horror. /Is there no balm in Gilead, no physician there?/Why has no skin grown over their wound?"

DRAPED IN MOURNING

In 1861 Lincoln had leased his Springfield house to a prosperous railroad man named Lucian Tilton for $350 a year. Over the next four years the Tiltons allowed thousands of visitors to inspect the premises. When his old hometown learned of Lincoln's death, the house was quickly draped in heavy black crape, with Mrs. Tilton personally supervising the uniform spacing of rosettes and the precise drooping of fabric.

Of many such pictures made at the time, this is the sole photograph retained by the Lincolns. A carte de viste by Springfield photographer F. W. Ingmire, it is a sad companion piece to the family's carte of Lincoln, Tad, and Willie posing there in 1860.

Many neighbors felt certain that Lincoln's widow would soon return to the old house, but Mary rejected the "sordid" suggestion that she return to "*our shell*, of a house . . . from whence," she claimed, "as we were leaving its doors, en route to W——— my dear husband—told me, he would not carry me back there again."

PRESIDENT LINCOLN'S DOG.

LINCOLN HAD "LOVED HIS HORSE WELL"

Lincoln's next-door neighbor in Springfield remembered that "he kept his own horse, fed and curried it. . . . He loved his horse well." Lincoln's Springfield horse, Old Robin, outlived him, and after the assassination he was photographed several times, promoted to fame by the enterprising owner who purchased him from Lincoln in 1861.

THE DOG THEY LEFT BEHIND

Like the household furniture, the Lincolns' household pet, Fido, was left behind in Springfield when the Lincolns departed for Washington. The boys deposited Fido with playmates. This carte by F. W. Ingmire, labeled "President Lincoln's Dog," is likely one of the many commercially reproduced copies published after the assassination sparked demand for souvenirs associated with the martyred President. But the fact that it is the most battered of all the pictures from the family album suggests that careless young Tad may have owned this copy himself.

"SACRED
RESTING
PLACE"

Mary Lincoln wanted her husband buried here, but her old neighbors did not. Without her permission, they purchased a six-acre plot in downtown Springfield and proposed that a permanent Lincoln monument be built there instead of in the bucolic Oak Ridge cemetery outside the city, where Lincoln's body had been placed in a temporary receiving vault. Mary was convinced that "the beauty & retirement of the spot" would have made it her husband's personal choice, and that it would eventually "meet the approval of the whole civilized world."

Mary's intransigence created a furor in Springfield. "The people are in a rage about it," one resident wrote, "and all the hard stories that ever were told about her are told over again. She has no friends here." Unmoved, Mary handed down an ultimatum: without "a formal & written agreement that *the* Monument shall be placed over the remains of my Beloved Husband, In *Oak Ridge* Cemetery" she would transfer the body to Washington.

Springfield surrendered. What Mary called Lincoln's "sacred resting place—where all my thoughts centre," would remain where it was.

Sculptor Larkin Mead, winner of a $1,000 prize for design of a perma-

Total height 100 ft.   Base 17 ft

THE NATIONAL LINCOLN MONUMENT,
Erecting at Springfield, Ills.

DESIGNED BY
LARKIN G. MEAD.
(Copy right secured.)

PHOTOGRAPHED AT
THE NATIONAL GALLERY,
Springfield, Illinois.

nent tomb, created for it a heroic bronze statue of Lincoln. The entire monument cost $240,000, much of it funded by public donations.

The family's carte de visite of the monument, issued by the National Photographic Gallery of Springfield with a Mead copyright, purported to show the tomb as it was "erecting," but the carte looks heavily retouched, with the Lincoln statue little more than an artist's conception.

The family album also contained photographs of the entrance to the cemetery and the receiving vault where Lincoln was buried from 1865 until the monument's dedication nine years later. Mary paid at least two visits to Oak Ridge before the monument was finished, to see "the tomb which contains my All, in life." The companion carte here shows the entrance to the cemetery grounds.

"THE ENTRANCE" Oak Ridge Cemetery.

IDOL OF THE PEOPLE

This Alexander Gardner carte de visite from the family album was one of several photographs in circulation in the mid-1860s of the Lincoln statuette sculpted, probably from life, by teenage artist Vinnie Ream.

In 1866 Vinnie startled Washington by winning a $10,000 competition for a full-length statue of the martyred President for the Capitol Rotunda. Mary Lincoln, her jealousy undisguised, insisted that Vinnie was "a stranger to this great, good and christ-like man," and not even "familiar with the expression of his face." Editor Jane Grey Swisshelm further charged that Vinnie had won the congressional commission by placing some "busts on exhibition, including her own." Predicted Mary: "Nothing but a mortifying failure, can be anticipated, which will be a severe trial to the Nation & the World."

Undaunted, Vinnie sailed off to Europe, created the heroic marble statue there, and then "the little sculptor-girl" returned in triumph to "warm and universal applause" at the unveiling ceremonies in 1871 (see program opposite). That the Lincoln family preserved the carte of her statue from life, despite Mary's dislike for her and, later, Robert's dislike for the statue,

ABRAHAM LINCOLN.
By Vinnie Ream.

suggests strongly that even for his loved ones, in death Abraham Lincoln had ceased being merely father and husband—he had become an idol.

Sculptress Vinnie Ream lets her long curls flow over her artist's smock as she poses, carving tool in hand, alongside her bust of Lincoln for this postwar photograph. Note the draping on the sculpture; it is a cloth, dipped in a plaster solution, and placed on the bust for the benefit of the photographer, who evidently thought it insufficiently classical without it. (*Lloyd Ostendorf*)

YOUNG LAWYER

This cabinet photograph of twenty-five-year-old Robert T. Lincoln was taken by Jonathan Carbutt in Chicago in 1868, the year Robert married, settled into his first law firm, and confronted his mother's growing mania over money. Still years away from her rancorous break with Robert, Mary took special pleasure in the fact that her son rejected a law career in Springfield to take his chances in Chicago. "Robert," she huffed, "prefers a larger field."

Within this year, Robert would also become a father for the first time, prompting his mother to write with pride: "So, is he not, a young Papa? It is all the better I think for young men to settle down early."

Robert also attempted to quash the embarrassing lecture series his father's old law partner, William Herndon, was delivering at the time. Herndon alleged, among other things, that Abraham Lincoln had loved only the New Salem girl Ann Rutledge, not Mary. Herndon rebuked Robert and continued vilifying him for the rest of his life. "I think he's a d——d fool," he sputtered. "He has the insane rage of his mother without the sense of his father."

ROBERT'S WIFE AND FATHER-IN-LAW

Glimpsing his future son-in-law for the first time at Abraham Lincoln's inauguration in 1861, Iowa Senator James Harlan thought Robert Lincoln "well developed physically, a strong, healthy, resolute, sensible-looking fellow; without the slightest appearance of ostentation or family pride."

Seven years later, Robert was married to Harlan's daughter, Mary, in the senator's Washington home. "There were but few present," noted President Lincoln's old Secretary of the Navy Gideon Welles. "Young Lincoln has made my house his home when in Washington during the days of courtship. . . . Regard for his father made him always a welcome guest. . . . His deportment and character . . . always impressed me favorably."

Robert's engagement had been an open secret in Washington for several years; Miss Harlan had been his escort to his father's inaugural ball in 1865. The match had his mother's approval, but Robert warned his fiancée about his mother, saying, "I am likely to have a good deal of trouble in the future." The mother of the groom returned to the nation's capital to see her son married, even though, she confided, "the terror of having to proceed to *Washington* to witness it, almost overpowers me." At the ceremony, "ostentatious displays customary on such occasions" were eschewed because Mary considered herself still in mourning. Mary Harlan Lincoln was dressed in a "plain" but "exceedingly tasteful and rich" white silk and satin gown. Mary Todd Lincoln wore black but admitted later that her return to the city of painful memories was not as unpleasant as she had feared.

DESIGNER OF THE LINCOLN TOMB

Larkin Goldsmith Mead was the sculptor who won the "friendly competition of American artists" to design the Lincoln Monument at Springfield's Oak Ridge Cemetery (see earlier illustration). Born in New Hampshire and raised in Vermont, Mead served as an artist-correspondent for *Harper's Weekly* during the first year of the Civil War, then left for Italy, where he studied sculpture, married an Italian, and settled in Florence, for most of his life. Mary Todd Lincoln visited his studio while she was in Italy in 1871.

This Italian-made photograph of the sculptor was inscribed on the back: "With compliments to Mrs. Lincoln." Along with the companion pose of Mrs. Mead, it may have been presented to her as she toured Mead's studio, or given later to Robert's wife around the time Mead undertook twin relief portraits of the younger Mr. and Mrs. Lincoln (see next illustrations).

SCULPTED PORTRAITS OF ROBERT AND HIS WIFE

Robert, as one observer noted, looked "like his mother rather than his father." Not long afterward a Chicago *Tribune* journalist provided a rare description of his reclusive wife, Mary: "a slight, regular featured, delicate-faced lady, with very dark brown eyes...very simple and gracious in her manners." These descriptions come vividly to life in these family relics, cabinet photographs made about 1871, showing companion relief sculpture portraits of the young couple created by Larkin Mead, designer of the Lincoln tomb. Three sets of the original sculptures were made.

These photographs were made by the Ulke Brothers of Washington, two men who, in 1865, had been boarders in the Petersen House, where Lincoln died, and spent the long night of April 14, 1865, boiling water and carrying it to the President's bedside.

DAUGHTER-IN-LAW AND GRAND-DAUGHTER

Mary Harlan Lincoln poses with her firstborn child, Mary "Mamie" Lincoln, in this Davis & Sanford cabinet photograph, taken in New York about 1873. When new uncle Tad told his mother that the baby "must be a rare young lady," Mary Todd Lincoln took up her pen to inform her daughter-in-law: "I am also of his opinion."

For a while she also expressed deep if somewhat overbearing affection for Robert's wife. "You know you will always BE FIRST LOVE of daughters-in-law," she wrote to her in 1870, adding: "I often tell Tad I can scarcely flatter myself he will ever marry to suit me quite as well as dear Bob has done." Cabinet photographs like this one, which measured about 4 by 5½ inches, came into vogue in the 1870s, changing the shape and purpose of albums. With fewer pictures to a page, viewers became more selective about their collections.

DAVIS & SANFORD

FIFTH AVENUE · NEW YORK ·

HIS MOTHER'S COUSIN REMEMBERS TAD

"He is certainly very clever," Mary Todd wrote glowingly of her cousin John B. S. Todd, back in 1840. They remained on friendly terms for years thereafter; he was one of the few Todd relatives to stay uninterruptedly in Mary's good graces. This carte-de-visite photograph apparently shows Todd as he looked after the war and was surely given after Willie's death. He inscribed it solely to Tad from his home in "Dakota."

MARY LINCOLN DIED IN THIS WOMAN'S HOUSE

When she was released from the sanitarium to which Robert had committed her in 1875, Mary returned to live in the Edwards home, where she had lived her first years as a Springfield belle, and in whose parlor she had married her husband in 1842.

After spending month after month in her darkened room, Mary finally reconciled with her only surviving son. She died in Elizabeth's house on July 16, 1882, surrounded by the trunks of fancy goods she had been accumulating for years while claiming poverty.

"My dear Sister," as Mary came to refer to Elizabeth late in her life, was similarly camera-shy. "Have no photos of myself," Mrs. Edwards wrote to an author in 1887, adding: "Have had some, unwillingly taken." This carte is one of those rare poses. "At one time in my life," Mrs. Edwards pointed out, allowing the Todd vanity to surface, "I should not have been much ashamed to show my face."

TAD COMES HOME

Tad took ill on the journey home from a three-year sojourn in Europe with his mother. When this carte de visite was taken by Julius Ulke in Washington, probably on their return, he had only a few more months to live.

Tad's new lean look may have been caused by factors other than poor health and the distasteful institutional food of European boarding schools. "Mother took him to a dentist," brother Robert had reported in late 1868, "who said that his teeth should be gradually forced into a proper position by means of a spring frame set in his mouth." The device made Tad's chronically "bad habits of speech" even worse. Robert briefly placed him under the care of a speech therapist, who ordered the dental apparatus removed, probably leaving him comparatively hollow-cheeked. As he had done a decade before, Tad drew facial hairs on his likeness, in this case penciling in a mustache.

JULIUS ULKE, WASH., D. C.

LEISENRING BROS., - Artists, Mt. Pleasant, Iowa.

THE LAST PHOTOGRAPH OF TAD

A painfully thin Tad Lincoln is photographed with an unidentified companion in the unlikely pose of writing. In fact, Tad was almost a teenager before he knew his letters. The portrait, his last, was made by Leisenring Bros. in Mount Pleasant, Iowa, probably in late spring or early summer 1871 on a final visit to his brother Robert's in-laws—the home Robert's wife thought "so very restful." As the carte shows, Tad had his hair trimmed short for this final vacation.

"*Very very* dangerously ill," experiencing such difficulty breathing that he had to sleep sitting up, strapped to a chair, Tad died on July 15 at the age of eighteen. "As grievous as other bereavements have been," wrote his heartbroken mother, "not one great sorrow, ever approached the agony of *this*. My idolized & devoted son, torn from me, when he had bloomed into such a noble, promising youth."

PRESIDENT ARTHUR'S JOURNEY THROUGH WYOMING
AND THE NATIONAL PARK, AUGUST, 1883.

F. JAY HAYNES,
PHOTO., FARGO, D. T.

BRADY. PHOTO.   WASHINGTON D.C.

OUT WEST WITH PRESIDENT ARTHUR

Photo opportunities had not yet become a White House routine in the 1880s, when Robert T. Lincoln served as Chester Alan Arthur's Secretary of War. Nonetheless, when the President set off in the summer of 1883 on a camping trip through Yellowstone Park, his party included not only Indian guides, 75 mounted cavalryman, 175 pack animals, a famous general, and at least three of his Cabinet ministers, including Lincoln, but also frontier photographer F. Jay Haynes of Fargo, Dakota Territory.

Haynes took this and several other shots of the group in rustic poses, publishing the results captioned *President Arthur's Journey Through Wyoming.* Not that the Arthur expedition exposed itself to many dangers associated with rough camps. One reporter wrote that the biggest threat they faced was the "steep hills covered with loose stones" that made their feet hurt after hiking.

Arthur posed here with the fifty-two-year-old Civil War hero General Phillip Sheridan (seated second from left), Secretary of the Treasury Charles J. Folger, Postmaster General Walter Gresham, and Secretary of War Lincoln (seated second from right). Neither Lincoln nor Arthur, despite the wild surroundings, makes an attempt to hide the impressive watch chains that decorate their city-fed paunches. Around the time the picture was taken, a journalist described Robert as "a very good looking man, indeed, who just misses the right to be called handsome, having none of the gauntness of the martyr President." Robert owned a complete, bound set of the Haynes photographs, which his descendants preserved along with the other family pictures.

THE SONS OF GIANTS

Not once did Abraham Lincoln pose for a photograph with a member of his Cabinet. But a generation later, his son Robert (middle) sat for this intriguing, eight-by-nine-inch Brady portrait with Edgar T. Welles (right), the son of Lincoln's Secretary of the Navy, Gideon Welles; and Edwin Stanton, Jr. (left), son of Lincoln's Secretary of War. Three years after sitting for the February 1877 photograph, Robert became Secretary of War himself.

This is not a pose inspired solely by nostalgic sentiment, for these three sons of Civil War giants were intimate friends. When Robert and his bride journeyed from Washington to New York for their honeymoon, young Stanton and Welles accompanied them. Years later, when Robert brought his son's body home from England for burial in the Lincoln tomb, the only person who accompanied him to Oak Ridge was Edgar Welles.

ROBERT COMMEMORATES THE LINCOLN-DOUGLAS DEBATES

O n October 7, 1896, the thirty-eighth anniversary of the Lincoln-Douglas debate in Galesburg, Robert T. Lincoln journeyed back to that quiet Illinois college town for a commemorative celebration. There he gave his only address on the subject of his father.

This photograph by Galesburg "view artist" Allen A. Green shows Robert speaking, sandwiched between busts of Douglas and Lincoln. Neither the setting nor the event inspired Robert to flights of memorable rhetoric. "It would suit me far better to be a listener," he candidly admitted. And while he proceeded to allude to the "grateful emotions that overcome me on witnessing this demonstration of respect for my father," he offered no new insights into his life. "He knew that here he had many sympathizing friends," Robert declared, "but what would have been his feelings could he have known that after nearly forty years, after his work was done over thirty years, there would come together such a multitude as this to do him honor?" It was an intriguing question, but Robert ventured no answer. "It is for others and not for me to say," he proclaimed. On another occasion, Robert would admit he hated speaking in public to "a vast sea of human faces."

R BARON OF INDUSTRY

obert T. Lincoln looks every inch the prosperous railroad magnate in this studio photograph. Robert began his fourteen-year career as president of the Pullman Company in 1897. When Ida M. Tarbell met him that year for the first time, the muckraking journalist and future biographer of Abraham Lincoln "devoured him with my eyes," searching "his face and manners for resemblances" to his father. "There was nothing," Tarbell recalled. "He was all Todd, a big plump man perhaps fifty years old, perfectly groomed with that freshness which makes men of his type look as if they were just out of the barber's chair, the admirable social poise of the man who has seen the world's greatest and has come to be sure of himself." Years after it was taken, the "affectionate grandfather" autographed this copy and gave it to his granddaughter, Mary Lincoln Beckwith.

To Mary Lincoln Beckwith
from her Affectionate grandfather

April 30th 1913

Robert T. Lincoln

PULLMAN BUILDING
CHICAGO.

February 8th 1909.

Walter A. Townsend, Esq.,

Managing Editor, The Springfield Record,

Springfield, Ill.

Dear Sir:

In reply to your letter of Satur-
day, I must ask you to excuse me from sending
a photograph of myself for publication. Not
only have I nothing on hand that would be good
for that purpose, but I have a very great desire to avoid any such publication and have
furnished nothing whatever for that use.

Very truly yours,

Robt Lincoln

ON THE EVE OF A NEW CENTURY

Over the years, Robert sat for several formal photographs, each successive portrait testifying openly to a growing self-confidence—and an expanding waistline. But as the nineteenth century drew to an end, so did Robert's desire to pose for new pictures. Writing to a cousin who had requested his photograph in 1897, he replied that he had not sat for one in twelve years "and in that way keep out the vile newspaper cuts." Declining another such request, this time from one of the newspapers themselves, Robert gleefully replied that "it is one of the minor pleasures of life left to me that I can open the paper feeling sure that I am not to be confronted by a portrait of myself."

ROBERT'S "ANCESTRAL HOME"

Ever since the torrid Washington summer of 1863, when the sweltering heat drove Mary Todd Lincoln and her eldest son into the cool mountains of New England for relief, Robert had harbored an abiding love for the region. Many years later, his law partner built a summer cottage in Manchester, Vermont, and when Robert visited him there, his fondness for the area was rekindled.

Now a wealthy man, he built his own summer retreat in the community, a twenty-four-room Georgian revival manor house he named Hildene, taking up residence there in 1905. The main house, photographed here in winter, sat atop more than four hundred acres and offered a breathtaking view of a valley that lay between two dramatic mountain ranges. Robert built an observatory on the grounds and developed a passion for astronomy. He became active in local charities and served as president of the nearby country club.

Even when he grew older, his health racked by "nervous prostration" and other disorders, he returned each summer to his beloved Hildene "as usual."

Not long before Robert's death there in 1926, an aide to President Theodore Roosevelt had visited Abra-

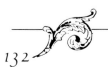

ham Lincoln's traditional birthplace log cabin in Kentucky, finding that it bore not only "the stamp of poverty" but of "degradation and uncleanliness" as well. If reports were true, he added, "that Bob Lincoln...does not relish the perpetuation of this cabin, I cannot blame him." Indeed, Robert himself confessed that he felt "like a stranger" in his old Midwest haunts. Perhaps that is why he came to refer to Hildene in faraway New England as his true "ancestral home."

ROBERT TEES OFF

"My daughter, Mrs. Isham, who is a very good photographer, has made several attempts at me on the golf course," Robert T. Lincoln wrote to a friend in 1910, "but she thinks I do not take as beautiful a picture as I used to do." Robert's letter enclosed one of Mamie's action poses, "which has at least the merit of not representing me in any lack of form in making a shot, which I am afraid would be my most characteristic attitude." This is probably the photograph to which the avid golfer referred, taken at the Ekwanok Country Club in Manchester, Vermont.

Not only did Robert play regularly at the Ekwanok, but he made an annual pilgrimage to Augusta, Georgia, for golf with such influential figures as Warren G. Harding and House Speaker Frederick H. Gillett. An observer nicknamed this group "the Little Mothers," explaining that "when the group came together it was for the purpose of rocking the cradle of the universe."

Sometimes Robert carried his love for the game to extremes. On frigid New Year's Day 1906, he took to the links in Chicago with his friend, retail magnate Marshall Field, and they played a full eighteen holes. Several days later, Field developed a sore throat, his condition worsened, and he died on January 16. Robert suffered a self-described "nervous break down" over the tragedy, and went to Augusta for a two-month rest.

This particular photograph was made into a postcard, which Robert may have sent to friends and family as a greeting from Hildene.

A PRESIDENT VISITS HILDENE

Toward the end of the acrimonious three-way presidential race of 1912, President William Howard Taft, soon to lose the White House to Woodrow Wilson, inexplicably suspended his campaign to embark with his wife on a vacation trip to New England. On October 10 he arrived in Manchester, and there he was put up at Hildene by Robert T. Lincoln. Lincoln and Taft shared a passion for golf, and the two played several times at Ekwanok. They also shared, by this time, a hatred of Theodore Roosevelt, one of Taft's challengers.

Taft gave a twenty-minute speech at the local hotel, where he was introduced to the seven hundred guests by Robert. The local newspaper could not resist reporting that the President had experienced considerable difficulty that night extricating himself from Robert's limousine, finding "no spare room in getting through the door way of the car."

Mr. and Mrs. Taft returned to Hildene the following summer. It was on one of these visits, in October 1912 or September 1913, that Taft and Lincoln posed for this photograph on the back terrace of Hildene, facing Robert's garden.

O
DEDICATING
THE LINCOLN
MEMORIAL

n May 30, 1922, seventy-nine-year-old Robert T. Lincoln made his final public appearance, at the dedication of the Lincoln Memorial in Washington. There the sixteenth President's son posed for this Harris & Ewing photograph with President Harding (left) and Speaker of the House Joseph Cannon, who believed Robert "one of the most misunderstood citizens of the country." At the glittering dedication ceremonies, President Harding and Chief Justice Taft, among others, delivered speeches, and poet Edwin Markham read a new version of his "Lincoln, Man of the People." But Robert said nothing, preferring that "no notice whatever" be taken of him. "Though second to none in admiration of his great father," the New York *Times* explained, "so many of the persons he met in life wanted to talk with him about President Lincoln that he early developed a reticence on that subject." Nor did Robert ever comment publicly on the Lincoln Memorial or the Daniel Chester French statue inside it.

THE FIRST LINCOLN GRANDCHILD

Mary Lincoln was wandering through Europe with Tad when her first grandchild, Mary, was born on October 15, 1869, "as fat and healthy as one could wish," her father reported joyfully. "I cannot realize," the widow wrote from Frankfurt a few months later, "that I am a *grandmama*— it appears to me, *at times,* so short a time, since my darling husband, was bending over me, with such love and tenderness—when the young father of that babe—was born."

Mary, inured to pessimism by life's recent hardships, was sure that the newest Lincoln would be named for someone other than herself. With both a mother and grandmother already named Mary, she admitted that "the child being called *so* too, would be rather too much in the beginning."

Mary Harlan Lincoln sent her mother-in-law this Jonathan Carbutt carte de visite of the newest Mary at seven and a half months, taken in Chicago, and signed in back (see illustration) by her father: "Miss Lincoln's compliments to Grandma."

Exile, though self-imposed, was painful: "That blessed baby," Mary said. "How dearly I would love to look upon her sweet young face." She would not until the baby was nearly two.

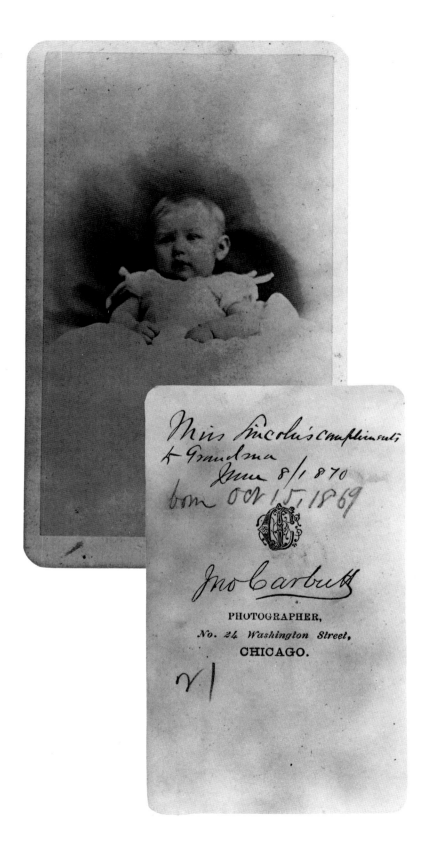

Cabinet Portrait
H. ROCHER   CHICAGO

"LITTLE MAMIE"

The youngest of the three Mary Lincolns—soon nicknamed Mamie—poses with her doll in this cabinet photograph by H. Rocher, taken in Chicago on February 1, 1874, when the child was four and a half. At the time this picture was taken, Mamie had become caught in the middle of Lincoln family conflict. Her grandmother's open denunciation of her mother, Robert sadly reported, had "driven my servants out of the room by her insulting remarks concerning their mistress & this in the presence of my little girl." A lady even told Robert that his mother "suggested . . . the idea of running away with the child."

Estrangement notwithstanding, Mary would soon fantasize about a new family of Lincolns returning in triumph to the White House—particularly her granddaughter, about whom she boasted: "*Little Mamie* with her charming manners & presence . . . will *grace* the place."

H. ROCHER · CHICAGO

THE THREE LINCOLN GRAND- CHILDREN TOGETHER

All three Lincoln grandchildren pose together for the W. P. Jordan cabinet photograph opposite, taken in Washington around 1883, when Robert was serving as Secretary of War. Jack was ten, Mamie (left) fourteen, and Jessie (right) eight. The photo below, showing Jack, Mamie, and Jessie posing in a studio prop boat, was taken by H. Rocher in Chicago some years earlier. These are two of the many cabinet photos in the family collection, a fine example of the style that supplanted the carte de visite in the early 1870s. As one photographer had declared before its introduction, noting that trade had become "dull": "The carte de visite, once so popular and in so great demand, seems to have grown out of fashion. Everyone is surfeited with them. All the albums are full of them, and everybody has changed with everybody . . . the adoption of a new size is . . . wanted . . . to create a fashion." The answer came from England, in the new 4-by-5½-inch cabinet images.

SUMMERING
IN IOWA

Mamie looks like a typical summer vacationer in this photograph by Leisenring's Studio in Mount Pleasant, Iowa, the town where her Harlan grandparents lived. Yet book, tennis racquet and sturdy-looking tree may well have been studio props.

When Mamie made her society debut in 1889, a newspaper wrote that "the granddaughter of Abraham Lincoln... has a bright, girlish face, in which there is no trace of the rugged features of her great ancestor." In fact, she resembled neither Lincoln nor Todd, but looked like her mother and the Harlan side.

Mamie's mother either accompanied or sent her children to Mount Pleasant nearly every summer between 1876 and 1888, because it was "so good for the children growing up."

Aside from Robert, there were more photographs, nearly forty altogether, of Mamie in the family collection than of any other Lincoln.

MAMIE'S WEDDING PORTRAIT

Mamie Lincoln was married to banking heir Charles Isham at the Gothic, ivy-covered Church of the Holy Trinity in Brompton Parish, near London, on September 2, 1891. "No members of London society" were on hand. Formal invitations had not been sent. Only sixty guests attended the ceremony —sister Jessie was not even asked to serve as a bridesmaid—and no more than forty came to the reception that followed at Ambassador Lincoln's home. Dressed in "white satin with a long train trimmed with orange blossoms and lace veil," Mamie struck an eyewitness as "a pretty, petite girl of sweet and winning nature . . . thoroughly well educated," but "not a bookish woman." Here she poses in her wedding gown for J. Thomson, photographer to the Queen. Her new husband was a cousin of Robert's law partner, Edward S. Isham. Described as "a ripe scholar," Charles Isham was librarian of the New-York Historical Society.

THE SECOND ABRAHAM LINCOLN

Not long after this carte was taken in 1880 or 1881, Abraham Lincoln II became a familiar sight at the White House as a playmate of President Garfield's son, Abram. Jack Lincoln, as he was known, developed a deep interest in the Civil War and liked to rehash the battlefield strategies of Grant and his grandfather's other generals.

He apparently also enjoyed mischievously imitating the distinctive signature of the man whose name he bore. Decades after his death, curators examining the books in Robert T. Lincoln's Hildene library were thrilled to discover many of them inscribed "A. Lincoln," assuming at first that they had belonged to the sixteenth President. Only when they noticed that most of the volumes had been published after President Lincoln's death did they realize that the autographing had been done by his imitative namesake, Abraham Lincoln II.

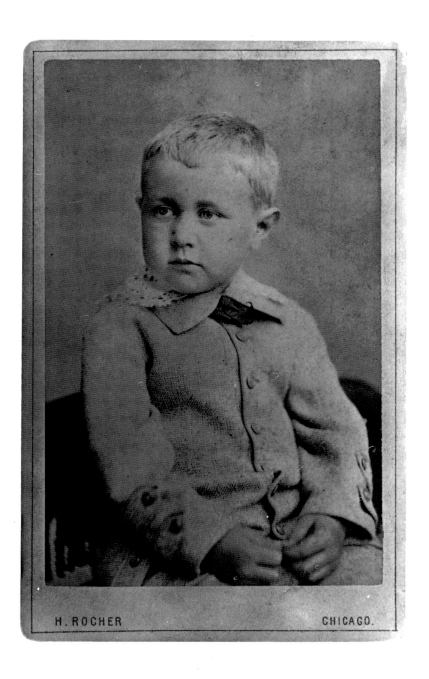

H. ROCHER   CHICAGO.

JACK AND ADMIRER

J ack Lincoln developed like most teenaged boys of his day. He liked baseball and sailing and, apparently, girls. Found in the family collection was this carte by Max Platz of Chicago, inscribed on the reverse: "To Jack with much love from Louise. September 21/89." Platz also took the vignetted photo of Jack, around 1889, when the young man was sixteen. There is no record of who "Louise" might have been.

A BOY AND
A BICYCLE

"**S**ecretary Lincoln has three children," noted *The Republic* in an 1881 "Celebrities at Home" feature on the Robert T. Lincoln family. "The second is a boy named Abraham, about eight years old, who rides a bicycle like a professional in company with the sons of President Garfield and Attorney General [I. Wayne] MacVeagh."

Jack posed with this large-wheeled vehicle a few years later. The boulder at left is a studio prop, as is the backdrop. Note the rolled-up portion of painted scenery at the bottom.

"THE MANLIEST BOY...I EVER KNEW"

"J ack' was a grave boy, deliberate in his speech and actions. He had much of the Lincoln blood in his veins." So one of his Chicago schoolteachers described him. But like the first Abraham Lincoln, Jack had a lighter side as well. Shown here dressed up in a serape, a big floppy hat, and thigh-high riding boots, he posed for Leisenring's Studio in Mount Pleasant astride a pony, just as his uncle Tad had posed in Washington years before.

As the boy's Chicago professor conceded, Jack was "up in athletics, and used to lead the boys in the playground." His father's law partner thought the boy was "unusually well developed for his age ... a large, strong fellow, with good muscles ... the manliest boy, I think I may say without exception, I ever knew."

THE LINCOLN NAME DIED WITH HIM

"I congratulate you most cordially in the recovery of your boy," lifelong friend John Hay wrote to Robert T. Lincoln at Christmastime 1889, around the time Abraham Lincoln II was photographed in bed for this candid Kodak snapshot (see companion shot in color section). But ten weeks later, Jack was dead.

In deep mourning, Robert told Hay: "Jack was to us all that any father and mother could wish and beyond that, he seemed to realize that he had special duties before him. . . . I did not realize until he was gone how deeply my thoughts of the future were in him."

An excellent student, Jack was being groomed to follow his father into Exeter, Harvard, and the law.

JESSIE LINCOLN BECKWITH JOHNSON RANDOLPH

"My experience with girl babies makes me envy him," Robert T. Lincoln wrote when a friend's wife gave birth to a daughter. "They are very nice." Of Robert's own two daughters, Jessie was undoubtedly the nicer-looking. While Mamie, a beautiful child, seemed to grow plainer with the passage of time, Jessie blossomed as a teenager. One contemporary in Mount Pleasant described her as "a slender young girl, riding a horse around town." Here the chic Jessie poses for a formal photograph dressed in the height of fashion, exaggerated puff-sleeved dress and ornate feathered hat.

GRAND-DAUGHTER AND GREAT-GRANDSON

Lincoln Isham was the only child of Mary "Mamie" Lincoln Isham, Robert's firstborn daughter. Until this

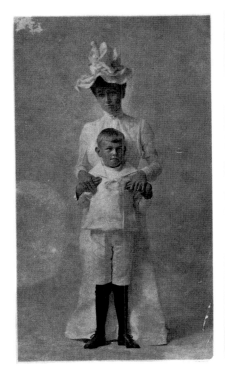

picture from the family album (left) became available to the public, there was no way to know that as a youth he had crossed eyes. When mother and son struck a similar pose (right) for a photographer some years later, Lincoln Isham had bloomed into a handsome young man—with his eyes, obviously corrected by surgery, bearing no trace of the condition.

LINCOLN ISHAM

Lincoln Isham died in Vermont in 1971 at the age of seventy-nine, leaving some $500,000 in personal property and real estate, not to mention the hefty residue of his father's banking fortune. Since the Ishams had no children together, more than $400,000 went to his stepdaughter and another $600,000 was left to friends and employees. To the Smithsonian, to which he had already presented his great-grandmother Mary Todd Lincoln's watches, Isham willed settings from the White House china service and a rather mundane portrait of President Lincoln by Kenyon Cox.

PEGGY
AND BOB
BECKWITH

Jessie Beckwith's children, Peggy and Bob, pose together in this studio photograph. In later years, sister and brother were only occasionally photographed by news photographers and friends. Generally, as one newspaper would report in 1931, they refused "point blank, though very politely, to allow a photographer to visit them."

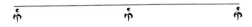

PEGGY
WITH
HER PET

Peggy Beckwith poses with her dog in this formal portrait, an expression of undisguised misery in the child's eyes. Crowned with an adorable Buster Brown haircut, Peggy was frequently trotted out to the photographers in her early years for pictures that showed her reading books and posing in staged rigidity with toys and pets.

THE BECKWITH FAMILY

When this charming family portrait was taken around 1912, Peggy Beckwith (left) was fourteen, and Bob eight. Their mother, Jessie, was approaching forty. At the time, Jessie had been divorced from Warren Beckwith for five years. She divorced a second husband, Frank E. Johnson, in 1925 and married her third, Robert J. Randolph, in 1926. Bob wears a sailor suit, a popular fashion of the day inspired by the competition in navy-building among the great powers before World War I.

BOB IN SUNNY ITALY

Bob Beckwith holds a parasol to shield him from the Italian sun in this candid snapshot taken in the late 1920s by a Venetian photographer named Giacomelli, but marked on the back, in ink: "Florence." The intimate inscription, "Lovingly, Bob," and its discovery in the family collection at Hildene strongly suggest it was sent to his family from a European holiday.

A newspaperman described Robert Todd Lincoln Beckwith some years later as "but 5 feet, 5 inches tall," with "hazel-grey eyes, a round face, and . . . heavy set."

PEGGY AT HILDENE

This Mary Lincoln Beckwith pose (top far right) was taken in the dining room of Hildene, beneath an oil portrait of her grandfather Robert. A newspaper of the day described Peggy as "the typical American girl, a natural sportswoman, who is interested in golf, flying, and loves the out-of-doors," a woman of "medium height,

with blue eyes and fair hair and complexion." On Lincoln's Birthday 1930, a local newspaper reported that this "level-headed woman of great ability and plenty of common sense" had taken up aviation.

REFIGHTING THE CIVIL WAR

For generations, Civil War Round Tables, North as well as South, have been cheerfully refighting the Civil War at meetings, banquets, reenactments, and symposia. The setting of this photograph is not identified, but Bob Beckwith is shown addressing one such gathering.

In 1933 Robert attended the seventieth anniversary of the Gettysburg Address, where he posed for the newspapers with the descendants of Grant and Lee, and in 1965 he traveled to Springfield for ceremonies marking the centennial of his great-grandfather's assassination. But these occasions proved the exception, not the rule. Asked by an interviewer why he never asked grandfather Robert what life had been like in the Lincoln White House, he shrugged and replied, "I was not especially interested."

THE LAST
OF THE
LINCOLNS

Mary Lincoln "Peggy" Beckwith died at age seventy-seven in 1975. Robert Todd Lincoln Beckwith died at eighty-one on Christmas Eve, ten years later. Neither left an heir; thrice-married Bob fathered no children, and Peggy remained single. When they died, Abraham Lincoln's direct line of descent came to an end. Asked during the Civil War centennial for her personal insights into the life of her great-grandfather, Peggy Beckwith spoke volumes with but nine words that neatly summed up the enormous gap between the generations in this famous family. Said one of the last Lincolns: "I'm as far away from him as anyone else."

NOTE ON PHOTOGRAPHIC SOURCES

Unless otherwise noted, all the photographs reproduced in this volume are from the collection of the Louis A. Warren Lincoln Library and Museum in Fort Wayne. The photographs on the bottom of page 149, the top of page 150, pages 152–53, and page 154 are all from family album originals now in the Illinois State Historical Library in Springfield, as are the illustrations of the album cover and album leaf on pages 41 and 51. The fragment from Lincoln's 1859 autobiographical sketch on page 53 is courtesy of the Library of Congress. The program reproduced on page 117 is courtesy of the Architect of the Capitol. And the material from artist Francis B. Carpenter's scrapbook on pages 100 and 104 is from the artist's descendant, Lawrence Ives.

NOTES TO INTRODUCTION

1. Elizabeth Todd Grimsley, "Six Months in the White House," *Journal of the Illinois State Historical Society,* 19 (October 1926–January 1927), 58.

2. William C. Darrah, *Cartes de Visite in Nineteenth Century Photography* (Gettysburg, Pa.: William C. Darrah, 1981), 4.

3. These original albums in Illinois State Historical Library. The Prince of Wales visited Lincoln's hometown, Springfield, Illinois, on September 26, 1860, but Lincoln decided it would be undignified to see him. See New York *Herald,* October 20, 1860.

4. William A. Welling, *Photography in America: The Formative Years, 1839–1900* (New York: Thomas Y. Crowell, 1978), 150.

5. E. & H. T. Anthony & Co., advertisement in *Harper's Weekly,* May 6, 1865, 286.

6. Carl Schurz, *The Reminiscences of Carl Schurz,* 3 vols. (New York: McClure & Co., 1908), II:188.

7. Gail Buckland, "From Royal Albums: Queen Victoria and Her Descendants Collected Photographs of What Interested Them," *The Connoisseur* (March 1987), 74.

8. Roy P. Basler et al., eds., *The Collected Works of Abraham Lincoln,* 9 vols. (New Brunswick, N.J.: Rutgers University Press, 1953–55), IV:39.

NOTES TO TEXT

1. Justin G. and Linda Levitt Turner, *Mary Todd Lincoln: Her Life and Letters* (New York, Alfred A. Knopf, 1972), 66.

2. Benjamin P. Thomas, *Abraham Lincoln: A Biography* (New York: Alfred A. Knopf, 1952), 464; Turner, *Mary Todd Lincoln*, 187, 200.

3. Turner, *Mary Todd Lincoln*, 285.

4. Ibid., p. 58; "Celebrities at Home," *The Republic*, 277 (imperfectly identified clipping from the Illinois State Historical Library, Springfield).

5. Turner, *Mary Todd Lincoln*, 200.

6. Ibid., 66, 82.

7. Roy P. Basler et al., eds., *The Collected Works of Abraham Lincoln*, 9 vols. (New Brunswick, N.J.: Rutgers University Press, 1953–55), VII:512; Mark E. Neely, Jr., and R. Gerald McMurtry, *The Insanity File: The Case of Mary Todd Lincoln* (Carbondale: Southern Illinois University Press, 1986), 174.

8. Harry J. Carman and Reinhard H. Luthin, *Lincoln and the Patronage* (New York: Columbia University Press, 1943), 114–15.

9. Francis B. Heitman, *Historical Register and Dictionary of the United States Army, from . . . 1789, to 1903*, I:399, 999, 589, 964.

10. Roy P. Basler, *President Lincoln Helps His Old Friends* (Springfield, Ill.: Abraham Lincoln Association, 1977) provides the fullest treatment of the subject. On the Edwards imbroglio, see *Collected Works of Lincoln*, VI:275.

11. Lockwood M. Todd to John Blair Smith Todd, October 16, 1861; Lockwood M. Todd to John Blair Smith Todd, December 5, 1861, Abraham Lincoln Papers, Library of Congress (microfilm).

12. Quoted in Lockwood M. Todd to John Blair Smith Todd, December 5, 1861.

13. Lockwood M. Todd to Abraham Lincoln, June 22, 1862 Abraham Lincoln Papers; Milton H. Shutes, *Lincoln and California* (Stanford, Calif.: Stanford University Press, 1943), 67–69.

14. Howard R. Lamar, *Dakota Territory, 1861–1889: A Study in Frontier Politics* (New Haven, Connecticut: Yale University Press, 1956), 53, 65, 67–68, 74, 91.

15. Turner, *Mary Todd Lincoln*, 85; *Collected Works of Lincoln*, IV:345; V:242.

16. William Nelson to John Blair Smith Todd, April 18, 1861, April 23, 1861, Abraham Lincoln Papers.

17. *The War of the Rebellion: A Compilation of the Official Records of the Union and Confederate Armies*, 128 vols. (Washington: Government Printing Office, 1880–1901), I:17, pt. 2, 117.

18. Lamar, *Dakota Territory*, 91.

19. *Collected Works of Lincoln*, IV:303; the letter was written to Democrat John Todd Stuart, who, if ill disposed, might have given it to the Democratic press to use against Lincoln. It seems proof of the trust between these two men that the President would write such a letter to a man who was a politician and not a Republican. Turner, *Mary Todd Lincoln*, 105.

20. *Official Records*, III:4, 465–66.

21. Turner, *Mary Todd Lincoln*, 180.

22. Turner, *Mary Todd Lincoln*, 464–65. Sarah was illiterate, but others in her proximity could read letters aloud to her.

23. Ibid., 130.

24. Emanuel Hertz, *The Hidden Lincoln: From the Letters and Papers of William H. Herndon* (New York: Viking, 1938), 177.

25. Turner, *Mary Todd Lincoln*, 61.

26. Benjamin B. French, quoted in *Mary Lincoln: Biography of a Marriage* (Boston: Little, Brown, 1953), 264.

27. Ibid., 82; George B. Forgie, *Patricide in the House Divided: A Psychological Interpretation of Lincoln and His Age* (New York: W. W. Norton, 1979), 170.

28. Edward Everett, *Orations and Speeches on Various Occasions*, 4 vols. (Boston: Little, Brown, 1868), IV:49–50; Dorothy T. Muir, *Presence of a Lady: The Story of Mount Vernon During the Civil War* (Mount Vernon: Mount Vernon Ladies' Association, 1974), 21.

29. Paul M. Angle, ed., *Herndon's Life of Lincoln*, orig. ed. 1885 (Cleveland: World Publishing, 1965), 386; *Collected Works of Lincoln*, IV:341.

30. Neely and McMurtry, *The Insanity File*, 180; Turner, *Mary Todd Lincoln*, 426, 67 and n.

31. Turner, *Mary Todd Lincoln*, 189.

32. John G. Nicolay and John Hay, *Abraham Lincoln: A History*, 10 vols. (New York: Century, 1890), IV:151–52; Turner, *Mary Todd Lincoln*, 86, 94.

33. Turner, *Mary Todd Lincoln*, 89.

34. John E. Washington, *They Knew Lincoln* (New York: E. P. Dutton, 1942), 105–26.

35. Jean H. Baker, *Mary Todd Lincoln: A Biography* (New York: W. W. Norton, 1907), 216; Turner, *Mary Todd Lincoln*, 189.

36. Turner, *Mary Todd Lincoln*, 128.

37. Ibid., 268, 273.

38. Ibid., 258.

39. Francis B. Carpenter, *Six Months at the White House with Abraham Lincoln* (New York: Hurd and Houghton, 1866), 93; Turner, *Mary Todd Lincoln*, 263, 273.

40. Turner, *Mary Todd Lincoln*, 250, 264, 399.

41. Ibid., 591 n.

42. Ibid., 250; Neely and McMurtry, *The Insanity File*, 5.

43. Turner, *Mary Todd Lincoln*, 260, 263.

44. Ibid., 482, 522; Neely and McMurtry, *The Insanity File*, 36.

45. Turner, *Mary Todd Lincoln*, 615–16.

46. Robert T. Lincoln to ————, June 28, 1887, Louis A. Warren Lincoln Library and Museum, Fort Wayne, Indiana.

47. "Highest Office was 'Prison' to Robert Lincoln," unidentified newspaper clipping, Louis A. Warren Lincoln Library and Museum.

48. Paul M. Angle, ed., *A Portrait of Abraham Lincoln in Letters by His Oldest Son* (Chicago: Chicago Historical Society, 1968), 7 and n., 47; Turner, *Mary Todd Lincoln*, 414, 416, 566.

49. Angle, *Portrait of Abraham Lincoln*, 24, 27, 29.

50. Baker, *Mary Todd Lincoln*, 310, 405 n.

51. Lincoln Isham, last will and testament, photocopy, Illinois State Historical Library; Flora G. Orr and Edith Porter, "Lincoln's Living Descendants," Washington *Star*, February 8, 1931, clipping in Louis A. Warren Lincoln Library and Museum.

52. Unidentified clipping in Louis A. Warren Lincoln Library and Museum; see also Baltimore *News*, November 12, 1929, clipping in Louis A. Warren Lincoln Library and Museum, and Washington *Star*, December 22, 1929, clipping in Illinois State Historical Library.

53. Herman Blum, "The Three Living Lincoln Descendants," Philadelphia *Evening Bulletin*, February 12, 1968; *The Banner*, Vol. 63, No. 4 (July–August 1959), clippings in Louis A. Warren Lincoln Library and Museum.

54. "Bobby Kennedy Goes Too Fast, Says Lincoln Kin," "Lincoln's Descendant Opposed to Aggressive Desegregation," Cincinnati *Post & Times-Star*, February 12, 1963; clippings in Louis A. Warren Lincoln Library and Museum.

55. Richard N. Frost, *Lincoln's Legacy* (Chicago: Aquarius Rising Press, 1989), 68.

56. Mary Lincoln Beckwith, last will and testament, photocopy in Illinois State Historical Library.

57. "Lincoln's Last Descendant Dies," Madison (Wisconsin) *Courier*, December 26, 1985, clipping in Louis A. Warren Lincoln Library and Museum.

58. "Lincoln's Great Grandson in City; Arrested for Speeding," Omaha *World-Herald*, September 8, 1925, clipping in Illinois State Historical Library.

59. Orr and Porter, "Lincoln's Living Descendants."

60. "Lincoln's Great-Grandchild Involved in Paternity Suit Here," Williamsburg (Virginia) *Gazette*, July 25, 1969; Kenneth Walker, "Lincoln Descendancy at Stake in Adultery Trial," Washington *Star*, April 3, 1976; clippings in Louis A. Warren Lincoln Library and Museum.

61. Lincoln College Bicentennial Convocation Program, December 1976, in Louis A. Warren Lincoln Library and Museum; "President Greets Lincoln Descendant," Illinois State *Register*, February 11, 1953, clipping in Illinois State Historical Library; "Lincoln Scion Doubts Value of Documents," Washington *Post*, July 12, 1947, clipping in Louis A. Warren Lincoln Library and Museum; and Louise Hutchinson, "102 Years After Lincoln Died: A Call on His Great-Grandson," Chicago *Tribune*, April 16, 1967, clipping in Louis A. Warren Lincoln Library and Museum.

62. Madison (Indiana) *Courier*, December 26, 1985, clipping in Louis A. Warren Lincoln Library and Museum.

63. Louise Hutchinson, "102 Years After Lincoln Died: A Call on His Great-Grandson."

NOTES TO CAPTIONS

Page

41 William Welling, *Photography in America: The Formative Years, 1839–1900*
(New York: Thomas Y. Crowell, 1978), 169–70.

42 Roy P. Basler et al., eds., *The Collected Works of Abraham Lincoln*, 9
vols. (New Brunswick, N.J.: Rutgers University Press, 1953–55), IV:114;
Frederick Hill Meserve and Carl Sandburg, *The Photographs of Abraham
Lincoln* (New York: Harcourt, Brace & Co., 1944), 7–8.

43 Rufus Rockwell Wilson, ed., *Lincoln Among His Friends* (Caldwell, Ida.:
Caxton Printers, 1942), 96–97; John S. Goff, *Robert Todd Lincoln: A
Man In His Own Right* (Norman, Okla.: University of Oklahoma Press,
1969), 22–23; Robert Todd Lincoln to Daniel Fish, 1919, Robert Todd
Lincoln Papers, Illinois State Historical Library.

44 Goff, *Robert Todd Lincoln*, 26; Rufus Rockwell Wilson, ed., *Intimate
Memories of Lincoln* (Elmira, New York: Primavera Press, 1945), 216–17;
Justin G. and Linda Levitt Turner, *Mary Todd Lincoln: Her Life and
Letters* (New York: Alfred A. Knopf, 1972), 634.

45 Katherine Helm, *The True Story of Mary, Wife of Lincoln* (New York:
Harper & Brothers, 1928), 115; Turner, *Mary Todd Lincoln*, 46, 53;
Floyd and Marion Rinhart, *The American Daguerreotype* (Athens: University of Georgia Press, 1981), 294.

46 Emanuel Hertz, *The Hidden Lincoln: From the Letters and Papers of
William H. Herndon* (New York: Viking, 1938), 129, 176–77.

47 Welling, *Photography in America: The Formative Years, 1839–1900*, 178;
Earl Schenck Miers et al., eds., *Lincoln Day by Day: A Chronology,
1809–1865*, 3 vols. (Washington: Lincoln Sesquicentennial Commission,
1960), III:143; Ward H. Lamon, *The Life of Abraham Lincoln* (Boston:
James R. Osgood, 1872), 469.

Page

48 John Hay, "Tad Lincoln," Springfield *Daily State Journal*, July 21, 1871, 2.

49 Goff, *Robert Todd Lincoln*, 194–96; South Norwalk (Connecticut) *Evening Sentinel*, February 7, 1922, clipping in Louis A. Warren Lincoln Library and Museum; Peter Pollack, *The Picture History of Photography*, rev. ed. (New York: Harry N. Abrams, 1969), 234–36.

53 Charles Hamilton and Lloyd Ostendorf, *Lincoln in Photographs: An Album of Every Known Pose*, rev. ed. (Dayton, Ohio: Morningside Books, 1985), 30; Herbert Mitgang, ed., *Abraham Lincoln: A Press Portrait* (Chicago: Quadrangle Books, 1971), 140; *Lincoln Day by Day*, II:262; Hertz, *The Hidden Lincoln*, 414.

54–55 Harry E. Pratt, *The Personal Finances of Abraham Lincoln* (Springfield, Ill.: Abraham Lincoln Association, 1943), 63–66; "A Lincoln: His House," *Lincoln Centennial Association Papers* (1925), 28–29; *Frank Leslie's Illustrated Newspaper*, March 9, 1861; Utica *Morning Herald*, June 27, 1860; Hamilton and Ostendorf, *Lincoln in Photographs*, 58–59.

55 Jean H. Baker, *Mary Todd Lincoln: A Biography* (New York: W. W. Norton, 1987), 48–51; Hertz, *The Hidden Lincoln*, 373–74; 376; Turner, *Mary Todd Lincoln*, 105.

56 "Recollections of a Springfield Doctor," *Journal of the Illinois State Historical Society*, 47 (Spring 1954), 59–60; Baker, *Mary Todd Lincoln*, 132.

57 Helm, *Mary Lincoln*, 15, 155–56, 180–81; Turner, *Mary Todd Lincoln*, 106.

58 Mark E. Neely, Jr. *The Abraham Lincoln Encyclopedia* (New York: McGraw-Hill, 1982), 178; Lamon, *Life of Abraham Lincoln*, 474; Turner, *Mary Todd Lincoln*, 598–99.

59 Wilson, ed., *Lincoln Among His Friends*, 96; Neely, *The Abraham Lincoln Encyclopedia*, 91; Jesse K. Dubois and David Davis to Abraham Lincoln, May 15, 1860, and Jesse K. Dubois to Abraham Lincoln, November 21, 1854, in Abraham Lincoln Papers, Library of Congress.

60–61 New York *World*, February 19, 1861; *Collected Works of Lincoln*, IV:129–30; Thomas D. Jones, *Memories of Lincoln* (New York: Press of the Pioneers, 1934), 14–15; Harold G. and Oswald Garrison Villard, eds., *Lincoln on the Eve of '61: A Journalist's Story by Henry Villard* (New York: Alfred A. Knopf, 1941), 49–50; *Collected Works*, IV:130; *Lincoln Day by Day*, III:16.

62 Harry W. Gourley to Robert T. Lincoln, February 22, 1861, Abraham Lincoln Papers, Library of Congress; Villard, *Lincoln on the Eve of '61*, 54–55; Elizabeth T. Edwards to Julia Edwards, in *Doris Harris Mail Auction Sale* (March 17, 1982); *Collected Works of Lincoln*, IV:82; New York *Herald*, March 5, 1861, in Ruth Painter Randall, *Lincoln's Sons* (Boston: Little, Brown, 1955), 70.

Page

64 William O. Stoddard, *Inside the White House in War Times* (New York: Charles L. Webster, 1890), 49; Grimsley, "Six Months at the White House," 47, 59; Donald B. Cole and John J. McDonough, eds., *Benjamin Brown French, Witness to a Young Republic: A Yankee's Journal, 1828–1870* (Hanover: University Press of New England, 1989), 382.

65 Tyler Dennett, ed., *Lincoln & the Civil War in the Diary and Letters of John Hay* (New York: Dodd, Mead, 1939), 172, 234, 241.

66 Wilson, *Intimate Memories of Lincoln*, 499; Villard, *Lincoln on the Eve of '61*, 55; Robert S. Harper, *Lincoln and the Press* (New York: McGraw-Hill, 1951), 86.

67 William O. Stoddard, *Abraham Lincoln: The True Story of a Great Life*, rev. ed. (New York: Fords, Howard, & Hulbert, 1884), 343–44; Helm, *Mary Lincoln*, 168.

68 *Collected Works of Lincoln*, IV:350; Helm, *Mary Lincoln*, 232.

69 John Hay, "Tad Lincoln"; Turner, *Mary Todd Lincoln*, 425.

70–71 Herbert Mitgang, ed., *Edward Dicey's Spectator of America* (Chicago: Quadrangle Books, 1971), 102; Turner, *Mary Todd Lincoln*, 185; Dennett, ed., *Hay Diary*, 17; *Collected Works of Lincoln*, IV:385–86.

72 Turner, *Mary Todd Lincoln*, 187, 499, 505, 588; *Collected Works of Lincoln*, VI:252, 358; Baker, *Mary Todd Lincoln*, 203.

74 F. Lauriston Bullard, *Lincoln in Marble and Bronze* (New Brunswick, N.J.: Rutgers University Press, 1962), 7.

75 New York *Herald*, March 28, 1861; April 3, 1862. Turner, *Mary Todd Lincoln*, 82; *Lincoln Day by Day*, III:104; Benson J. Lossing, *George Washington's Mount Vernon*, reprint of 1870 ed. (New York: Fairfax Press, n.d.), 369–70; *Collected Works of Lincoln*, VII:225.

76 *The War of the Rebellion: A Compilation of the Official Records of the Union and Confederate Armies*, 128 vols. (Washington: Government Printing Office, 1880–1901), I:5, 414–420.

77 Wilson, *Lincoln Among His Friends*, 97; Helm, *Mary Lincoln*, 168; Turner, *Mary Todd Lincoln*, 189, 250, 283; Wilson, *Intimate Memories of Lincoln*, 400.

78–79 Turner, *Mary Todd Lincoln*, 116, 189, 285; Ruth Painter Randall, *Mary Lincoln, Biography of a Marriage* (Boston: Little, Brown, 1953), 326; Lydia Maria Child to Sarah Shaw, December 15, 1861, in Louis A. Warren Lincoln Library and Museum; Hertz, *The Hidden Lincoln*, 376.

80–81 Turner, *Mary Todd Lincoln*, 94, 128, 268; *Lincoln Lore*, No. 332 (August 19, 1935); Allen Thorndike Rice, ed., *Reminiscences of Abraham Lincoln by Distinguished Men of His Time* (New York: North American Review, 1888), 469.

Page

82 Elizabeth Keckley, *Behind the Scenes* (New York: G. W. Carleton & Co., 1868), 132.

83 Turner, *Mary Todd Lincoln*, 306, 350, 360, 403, 546–47, 572; James R. Gilmore, *Recollections of Abraham Lincoln and the Civil War* (Boston: L. C. Page, 1898), 155.

84 Helm, *Mary Lincoln*, 108–9, 221, 224, 231–32; Theodore Calvin Pease and James G. Randall, eds., *The Diary of Orville Hickman Browning*, 2 vols. (Springfield: Illinois State Historical Library, 1925), I:651; *Collected Works of Lincoln*, VII:484–85; Neely, *Abraham Lincoln Encyclopedia*, 143.

85 *Collected Works of Lincoln*, IV:38; Francis B. Carpenter, *Six Months at the White House with Abraham Lincoln* (New York: Hurd & Houghton, 1866), 135.

86–87 Jay Monaghan, *Diplomat in Carpet Slippers: Abraham Lincoln Deals with Foreign Affairs* (Indianapolis: Bobbs-Merrill, 1945), 58, 137–38.

88–89 *Lincoln Day by Day*, III:168, 297–98; Keckley, *Behind the Scenes*, 122–24; Osborn H. Oldroyd, ed., *The Lincoln Memorial: Album-Immortelles* (New York: G. W. Carleton, 1882), 319.

90–91 Helm, *Mary Lincoln*, 212; Randall, *Mary Lincoln*, 325–26.

92–93 *Collected Works of Lincoln*, VII:544; John Hay, "Tad Lincoln"; Allen Thorndike Rice, ed., *Reminiscences of Abraham Lincoln by Distinguished Men of His Time* (New York: North American Review, 1888), 470.

94 Dennett, ed., *Hay Diary*, 117; Wilson, *Intimate Memories*, 406, 409.

95 Helm, *Mary Lincoln*, 227; *Collected Works of Lincoln*, VIII:223–24; Turner, *Mary Todd Lincoln*, 295.

96–97 *Lincoln Day by Day*, III:21–22, 25–26, 46–47; Robert W. Johannsen, *Stephen A. Douglas* (New York: Oxford University Press, 1973), 542–43; Turner, *Mary Todd Lincoln*, 298.

98 Carpenter, *Six Months at the White House*, 58–59; Wilson, ed., *Intimate Memories*, 402; William C. Darrah, *Cartes de Visite in Nineteenth Century Photography* (Gettysburg: W. C. Darrah, 1987), 24.

99 *Collected Works of Lincoln*, VI:326; Keckley, *Behind the Scenes*, 134; Turner, *Mary Todd Lincoln,* 518, 589.

100–5 Turner, *Mary Todd Lincoln*, 283–85, 298, 368; Harold Holzer, Mark E. Neely, and Gabor S. Boritt, "Francis Bicknell Carpenter (1830–1900): Painter of Abraham Lincoln and His Circle," *The American Art Journal* 16 (Spring 1984), 79–83.

106–7 Dennett, ed., *Hay Diary*, 79.

108–9 Richard J. Gutman and Kellie O. Gutman, *John Wilkes Booth Himself* (Dover, Mass.: Hired Hand Press, 1979), 27; Goff, *Robert Todd Lincoln*, 259; Roy Meredith, *The Face of Robert E. Lee in Life and Legend* (New York: Fairfax Press, 1981), 30–31; Keckley, *Behind the Scenes*, 135–36.

Page

110–11 Bloomington *Daily Pantagraph*, April 18, 1865.

112 Wayne C. Temple, *By Square and Compass: The Building of Lincoln's Home and Its Saga* (Bloomington, Ill.: Ashlar Press, 1984), 71; Dorothy Meserve Kunhardt and Philip B. Kunhardt, Jr., *Twenty Days* (New York: Harper & Row, 1965), 251, 254; Turner, *Mary Todd Lincoln*, 370.

113 Hertz, *The Hidden Lincoln*, 384; Hamilton and Ostendorf, *The Photographs of Abraham Lincoln*, 33; Randall, *Lincoln's Sons*, 65.

114–15 Turner, *Mary Todd Lincoln*, 244–45, 312, 384; Randall, *Mary Lincoln*, 387; Paul M. Angle, "The Building of the Lincoln Monument," *Lincoln Centennial Association Papers* (1926), 31, 36–37.

116–17 Gordon Langley Hall, *Vinnie Ream* (New York: Holt, Rinehart and Winston, 1963), 42, 44; Turner, *Mary Todd Lincoln*, 387, 416, 536; Hertz, *The Hidden Lincoln*, 238.

118 Helm, *Mary Lincoln,* 267; Goff, *Robert Todd Lincoln*, 91; Turner, *Mary Todd Lincoln*, 263–64, 370.

119 Helm, *Mary Lincoln*, 167, 268; Gideon Welles, *Diary*, 3 vols. (Boston: Houghton Mifflin, 1911), III:444; Turner, *Mary Todd Lincoln*, 481; Goff, *Robert Todd Lincoln*, 89.

120 Turner, *Mary Todd Lincoln*, 584; Bullard, *Lincoln in Marble and Bronze*, 54–55; Goff, *Robert Todd Lincoln*, 118–19.

121 Goff, *Robert Todd Lincoln*, 118; Chicago *Tribune*, May 31, 1884, ibid.; Kunhardt and Kunhardt, *Twenty Days*, 49, 53.

122 Turner, *Mary Todd Lincoln*, 505, 581, 583.

123 Ibid., 18; Hertz, *The Hidden Lincoln*, 376.

124 Goff, *Robert Todd Lincoln*, 94.

125 Louis Haselmayer, *The Harlan-Lincoln Tradition at Iowa Wesleyan College* (Mount Pleasant, Iowa: Iowa Wesleyan College, 1977), 19; Turner, *Mary Todd Lincoln*, 590, 596.

126 Goff, *Robert Todd Lincoln*, 89, 181, 196; Welles, *Diary*, III:444.

127 Goff, *Robert Todd Lincoln*, 122, 125, 141; New York *Times*, August 13, 1883; *Journey Through the Yellowstone National Park and Northwestern Wyoming*, Robert T. Lincoln's copy in Illinois State Historical Library.

128–29 *Speech of Hon. Robert T. Lincoln Made at the Celebration of the Thirty-eighth Anniversary of the Lincoln-Douglas Debate* (Hancock, N.Y.: Herald Printers, 1921); Randall, *Lincoln's Sons*, 58.

130 David C. Mearns, *The Lincoln Papers*, 2 vols. (Garden City, N.Y.: Doubleday, 1948), I:87–88.

131 Goff, *Robert Todd Lincoln*, 231–32.

132–33 Ibid., 235–36, 258–60, 262.

134 Robert T. Lincoln to Walter J. Travis, September 21, 1910, Robert Todd Lincoln Papers, Illinois State Historical Library; Goff, *Robert*

Page

Todd Lincoln, 235, 239–40; Nicholas Murray Butler, *Across the Busy Years: Recollections and Reflections*, 2 vols. (New York: Charles Scribner's Sons, 1939–40), I:379–80.

134 Manchester (Vermont) *Journal*, September 11, 1913, and October 10, 1912, clippings at Robert Todd Lincoln's Hildene, Manchester, Vt.; Goff, *Robert Todd Lincoln*, 240–41; William Howard Taft to Robert T. Lincoln, August 27, 1913, Hildene Collection.

135 Bullard, *Lincoln in Marble and Bronze*, 340–42; New York *Herald Tribune*, July 27, 1926, clipping in Louis A. Warren Lincoln Library and Museum; Goff, *Robert Todd Lincoln*, 262; Mearns, *The Lincoln Papers*, I:105.

136 Goff, *Robert Todd Lincoln*, 94; Turner, *Mary Todd Lincoln*, 522, 536, 580.

137 Neely and McMurtry, *The Insanity File*, 36; Turner, *Mary Todd Lincoln*, 684.

138–9 Welling, *Photography in America*, 185.

140 Unidentified newspaper clipping, February 13, 1889, Louis A. Warren Lincoln Library and Museum; Louis A. Haselmayer, *The Harlan-Lincoln Tradition at Iowa Wesleyan College*, 19.

141 *P.E.O. Record*, June 1988, 10–11.

142 Goff, *Robert Todd Lincoln*, 118, 194.

143 Ibid., 194.

144 *The Republic*, June 18, 1881, clipping in the Louis A. Warren Lincoln Library and Museum.

145 Chicago *Tribune*, February 25, 1890, and March 12, 1890; clippings in the Louis A. Warren Lincoln Library and Museum.

146–47 Goff, *Robert Todd Lincoln*, 195–96.

148 Ibid.,, 149; unidentified clipping in Louis A. Warren Lincoln Library and Museum.

149 Washington *Star*, February 8, 1931, clipping in Louis A. Warren Lincoln Library and Museum.

150 Ibid.

151 Guy Allison, "The Last of the Lincolns," Oakland *Tribune*, February 7, 1960.

152 Louise Hutchinson, "102 Years after Lincoln Died: A Call upon His Great-Grandson," Chicago *Tribune*, April 16, 1967; Oakland *Tribune*, February 7, 1960, clippings in Louis A. Warren Lincoln Library and Museum.

152–53 Unidentified clippings in Louis A. Warren Lincoln Library and Museum.

153 Chicago *Tribune*, April 16, 1968.

154 Unidentified clippings in Louis A. Warren Lincoln Library and Museum.

INDEX

ABOUT THE AUTHORS

Mark E. Neely, Jr., is the Director of the Louis A. Warren Lincoln Library and Museum in Fort Wayne, Indiana. He is the author of *The Abraham Lincoln Encyclopedia,* for which he won the Barondess/Lincoln Award, and coauthor of *The Insanity File: The Case of Mary Todd Lincoln.* He lectures frequently on Lincoln and contributes to many scholarly and historical publications. He is the recipient of a Lincoln Diploma of Honor from Lincoln Memorial University.

Harold Holzer has contributed articles about American historical prints and photographs to major magazines over the past fifteen years, including *Life, American Heritage,* and *American History Illustrated.* He is the recipient of the 1981 Barondess/Lincoln Award and of a Lincoln Diploma of Honor from Lincoln Memorial University. He is a member of the board of directors of the Abraham Lincoln Association and a founder of the Lincoln Group of New York.

Neely and Holzer are coauthors, with Gabor S. Boritt, of *The Lincoln Image* and *The Confederate Image.*

B O O K   M A R K

The text of this book was composed in
the typeface Cloister
with display typography in Antique Solid
by Jackson Typesetting Company
Jackson, Michigan

This book was printed in duotone
and four color process
by Mandarin Offset
Hong Kong

BOOK DESIGN AND ORNAMENTATION BY
CAROL A. MALCOLM

Abraham Lincoln   M. 1842   *Mary Todd*
1809~1865   1818~1882

Mary   M. 1868   *Robert Todd*   *Edward Baker*
Harlan   1843~1926   *"Eddie"*
                                               1846~1850

Charles   M. 1891   *Mary "Mamie"*   *Abraham II*
Isham   1869~1938   *"Jack"*
                                               1873~1890

Lincoln
Isham
1892~1971